WHAT PEOPLE ARE SAYING ABOUT *NO B.S. WEALTH ATTRACTION IN THE NEW ECONOMY*

"I am now implementing some of your techniques and wanted to let you know that the best piece of advice you gave me was [note: it's in this book, in Wealth Magnet 14] as of today, I have already gotten **over $60,000.00 in (in one week**)! I again want to thank you, I am grateful for your 'no B.S.' approach."

—David C. Gross, 144 Music And Arts Inc., www.144musicanarts.com, New York. David's company is a leader in the new, expanding field of outsourced teaching artists, providing professional musicians and artists as well as equipment to public schools on contract.

"Last week I celebrated my 50th birthday. After the party, I thought about how much I have to be thankful for. I thought of you immediately. I now have **more money than I'll probably need for the rest of my life.** So much of the credit for that goes to you. Yeah, I know money isn't everything, but money buys you freedom, and freedom is everything. Thank you so much."

—Paul Hartunian, paulhartunian.com, New Jersey. Paul is the leading authority on do-it-yourself publicity. He helps thousands of entrepreneurs obtain local and national print and broadcast media exposure, and has himself been on dozens of major talk shows including *The Tonight Show*, hundreds of radio programs, featured in *Forbes*, etc. He is "the man who sold the Brooklyn Bridge."

"You've helped us make money since 1993, and many of your ideas have earned us a small fortune."

—T. J. Rohleder, M.O.R.E. Inc., Kansas. T.J. is the owner of a giant publishing/mail-order business generating millions of dollars annually, started from scratch, with one simple idea and one advertisement.

"My friend Dan Kennedy is unique, a genius in many ways. I have always admired his ability to **see the vital truths in any business and to state these realities with straight language and clear definitions.** His approach is direct. His ideas are controversial. His ability to get results for his clients unchallenged. What you discover in the pages ahead will **change your business life and income forever."**

—Brian Tracy, www.briantracy.com. Brian is one of America's most sought after and popular professional speakers and the author of dozens of outstanding business books, including *Turbo Strategy: 21 Ways To transform Your Business*. This comment is from Brian's introduction to another book in the No B.S. series, *No B.S. Business Success*.

"After 8 or 9 years' association with Dan, I'm still learning . . . his ideas have **created millions and millions of dollars** of revenue for us."

—Ron LeGrand, www.globalpublishinginc.com. Ron is the author of *Quick-Turn Real Estate*, and is the #1 authority and "grand-daddy" of the entire industry of independent real estate entrepreneurs who buy and flip properties for big, fast profits. Virtually every other expert in this field has been a Ron LeGrand student. Ron has personally done thousands of real estate transactions and, combined with his students—many of whom have become millionaires in short time—turns over hundreds of millions of dollars of real estate every year.

For a larger collection of client and student comments about Dan Kennedy's work as well as information about his other books, newsletters, and services, visit these websites:

www.NoBSBooks.com

www.DanKennedy.com

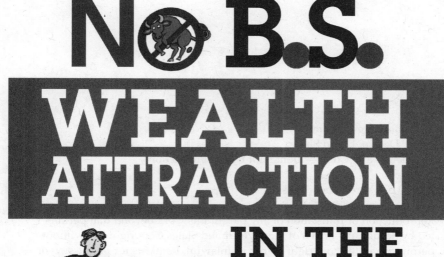

NO B.S.

WEALTH ATTRACTION

IN THE NEW ECONOMY

- Adapt to New Business Realities
- Gain Extreme Marketplace Advantage
- Profit From New Economy Customers

Dan S. Kennedy

EP
Entrepreneur.
Press

Publisher: Jere L. Calmes
Cover Design: David Shaw
Production and Composition: Eliot House Productions

This publication is designed to provide accurate and authoritative information in regard to the subject matter covered. It is sold with the understanding that the publisher is not engaged in rendering legal, accounting or
other professional services. If legal advice or other expert assistance is
required, the services of a competent professional person should be sought.

Library of Congress Cataloging-in-Publication Data
    Kennedy, Dan S., 1954–
      No bs wealth attraction in the new economy/by Dan Kennedy
        p.   cm.
      ISBN-10: 1-59918-369-2 (alk. paper)
      ISBN-13: 978-1-59918-369-5 (alk. paper)
      1. Success in business. 2. Entrepreneurship. 3. Wealth. I. Title.
    HF5386.K27655 2010
    658.15'224—dc22   2009033555

Printed in Canada
15 14 13 12 11 10   10 9 8 7 6 5 4 3 2 1

The old economy is shattered and gone forever.

It's never coming back as it was.

While some time-honored, reliable business strategies and skills continue to have their place—are even more important than ever— they must be combined with new, more creative and agile thinking and tough-minded and disciplined methods in sync with the realities of The New Economy and the demands of its consumers and clients.

Welcome to The New Economy

Well, it's not like we shouldn't have seen this coming.

Problem: We are monstrously over-stored. The same stores every few miles. The joke about Starbucks was it had reached the point where they were opening new Starbucks in the men's rooms in existing Starbucks. Me-too, same-as, indistinguishable chain stores and chain restaurants with zero differentiation right across the parking lot from one another. Simply much, much more than the market could support; implosion certain destiny.

Problem: There are far too many overlapping brands. Should there ever have been Cadillac pick-up trucks when GM also has Chevy and GMC trucks? Other than to perpetuate jobs locked in by union contract, could the existence of Pontiac *and* Buick *and* Chevy *and* Cadillac *and* GMC possibly be justified? This was not unique to GM, though—many other companies sinned similarly. And it seems everybody wanted to play in everybody else's sandbox, sacrificing their very identities to their detriment. Starbucks added egg, cheese, and meat breakfast sandwiches (that ruined the coffee aroma in their stores) while McDonalds hurried to add lattes and gourmet coffee while Subway added pizza while Dominos Pizza added sub sandwiches, your pharmacy added clothes and lawn furniture, Wal-Mart added iPhones. It's a damn mess that must be cleaned up.

Problem: Everybody already owns too much stuff. How many cars, TVs, computers, games, remodeled kitchens, and backyard decks can consumers consume before they need a break? Above all else, the recession was made and extended by demand problems.

Problem: Worst of all, salesmanship perished and service went to hell in a handbasket as free-flowing, easy, excess credit and the latest in a series of fools' bubbles (this one with theoretically never-ending multiplying of property values so homes became ATMs, not investments) enabled countless companies with poor sales practices, lazy and inept salespeople, sloppy over-staffing, casual management, and abysmal customer service to prosper—or at least seem to prosper. Truth is, consumers welcomed a good excuse to stay home and stop buying and punish.

Imagine a very loosely held together, giant ball of yarn with dozens of loose ends poking out all over the place. It wouldn't matter much which of the loose ends you gave a good tug; the entire ball, really just a pile of yarn, would implode and collapse and unravel. So it has been with the economy. It really wouldn't have mattered if it had been too many sub-prime mortgages issued to poorly qualified and irresponsible borrowers, based on inflated equity with no regard to the borrowers' ability to pay, then bundled together in inventive investment packages, or the sudden skyrocketing of gas prices, or the weight of mass-multiplied, poorly regulated hedge funds, or the accelerating disappearance of old-style manufacturing jobs sent overseas or just about any other loose end you might name—any one given a good yank would have been enough. Of course, what we witnessed were several getting pulled hard in different directions at the same time.

Incidentally, the real estate bubble was visible far, far in advance of its bursting. In 2003, an outstanding book on the subject, *The Coming Crash in the Housing Market* by John Talbott, a former vice-president at Goldman Sachs and real estate economist, very accurately predicted both the mortgage meltdown and real estate crash we've recently experienced. Reading it saved me some money. Authoritative articles began appearing pretty frequently from 2004 on, like the one on July

26, 2004, in the *Financial Times*, headlined "Party Over—Turn Off the Housing Boom Lights," which stated that "the end is near in use of exotic type mortgage money." We should have seen this coming. Some of us did. I began foretelling in earnest of 2007–08 in my *No B.S. Marketing Letter* and other publications in 2004.

What has been painfully revealed are extreme, systemic weaknesses and flaws and vulnerabilities—and gross excesses—throughout our socio-economic, financial, and political systems, papered over for a while, but worsening like undiagnosed disease all the while until, finally, we got slapped in the face with a monster recession. It's not my first rodeo. I built my first businesses during the Jimmy Carter recession, with tight credit, double-digit interest, inflation, and unemployment rates, gas shortages, and gas lines. These things may very well be avoidable, but they happen. For people seeing it firsthand for the first time, it is terrifying and can be paralyzing. But it's not the first time and it won't be the last time traumatic change has replaced an old economy with a New Economy.

In The New Economy, it may very well be harder to attract wealth than it has been in recent years.

There has been a great deal of talk by economists, futurists, financial analysts, politicians, and the media about the need to lower our expectations and shrink our lifestyles as the only rational response to all that has occurred, in the United States and globally, in 2008, 2009. An article in *USA Today*, for example, warned of the need to "brace for a lower standard of living." The President has suggested this as well. Unfortunately, I suppose it may very well be valid advice for those who accept it, for those who routinely accept governance by circumstances.

But for you and I, lowering expectations is the least rational response I can think of. It only makes sense if you wish to cede control of your life to circumstances. That is a fundamental choice that belongs exclusively to you.

There are, of course, changed and changing facts and realities in the business and financial landscape, but a good way to think about them is as a pro football team's coaches and players must think about games played on natural turf, artificial turf, outdoors, indoors, in heat, in cold, in rain, in snow—regardless, they play to win. And *somebody* does, every time. I drive harness racing horses and we race in good and foul weather, outdoors, year-round. In the last ten years, a night of racing at the track where I drive has been post-poned and re-scheduled only twice, due to violent ice storms and blizzards. Given the differing weather and track conditions, you plan your race strategy differently, you may condition your horse differently during the week, you may equip him differently on race night, you may dress differently, and you may need to steel yourself mentally for bitter cold or pouring rain and mud. But you do not set aside your intentions of winning.

Whatever the realities are, one is that there is wealth. As long as it exists, it is yours to attract, by combining the right thinking, strate-gies, actions, and behaviors.

Some of the BIG IDEAS in this Book that Will Challenge You

How to experience **The Phenomenon**—attract more wealth in the next 12 months than in the previous 12 years!

Do you suffer from **Wealth Inhibition**?

You do **not** get what you deserve.

The **difference** between the wealthy entrepreneurs and the also-rans is *not* as great as most believe.

Positive Thinking alone is **worthless**.

What is your **#1** Entrepreneurial Responsibility?

Is there a **"dirty little secret"** behind many wealthy entrepreneurs?

The **worst** of all wealth-defeating habits is . . .

YCDBSOYA

Are you an "opportunity thinker"—or are you **guilty** of "outcome thinking"?

"Do what you love and the money will follow" is **B.S.** hazardous to your wealth.

Stop playing **Blind Archery**

12 Ways To Increase Your "**Personal** Value"

Why you must **STOP thinking about Income!**

You need your own **Zero Tolerance Policy** about . . .

The 90-Day Experiment that may change your life forever.

Contents

Acknowledgments, xvi

PREFACE

How To Make Yourself Magnetic to Money xvii

Book Roadmap, xxii

SECTION I
WEALTH MAGNETS

WEALTH MAGNET 1

No Guilt. 3

A Tale of Two Teenagers, 4

WEALTH MAGNET 2

Unequivocal Belief In Abundance 15

Don't Buy What the Bad Newsmongers Are Selling, 21

WEALTH MAGNET 3

Break Free of "Fairness" 27

WEALTH MAGNET 4

Accepting Your Role and Responsibilities 34

Are You "Guilty" of Opportunism?, 38

WEALTH MAGNET 5

No Fear. 41

WEALTH MAGNET 6

No Excuses 48

Pressure–Prosperity Link, 54

WEALTH MAGNET 7

Speak Money. 59

What You Speak Reveals What You Are, 65

WEALTH MAGNET 8

Be Somebody 69

Be an Expert Somebody, 72

WEALTH MAGNET 9

Be Somewhere 76

WEALTH MAGNET 10

Do Something 81

WEALTH MAGNET 11

Demonstration. 94

WEALTH MAGNET 12

Follow-Up 108

Beware the Gold Star Syndrome, 109
Why Is Follow Up So Magnetic?, 112

WEALTH MAGNET 13

Integrity 114

WEALTH MAGNET 14

Ask 117

WEALTH MAGNET 15

Domino Opportunity 120

WEALTH MAGNET 16

Passion 123

WEALTH MAGNET 17

See What Isn't There 127

WEALTH MAGNET 18

No Boundaries 136

WEALTH MAGNET 19

Clarity 141

WEALTH MAGNET 20

Independence 146

WEALTH MAGNET 21

Think Value, Not Time 150

WEALTH MAGNET 22

Think Equity, Not Income 155

WEALTH MAGNET 23

Marketing Prowess 159

WEALTH MAGNET 24

Behavioral Congruency 163

WEALTH MAGNET 25

Act Wealthy to Attract Wealth 168
   The Power of Habitforce, 171

WEALTH MAGNET 26

Energy From People 175
   How To Build a "Power Team" Around You, 178

WEALTH MAGNET 27

Courage 181

WEALTH MAGNET 28

Pace 184

SECTION II
BONUS CHAPTERS

How a Small University Went from
   Stodgy to Spectacular Using
   Wealth Attraction Magnets 195
   The Renaissance at High Point, 198

The Reinvention of the Barbershop
with Wealth Attraction 206
   Shave and a Haircut, Not Two Bits, 209

It's No Wonder He's So Successful. Look At 219

SECTION III
WEALTH RESOURCES

Bank of Wealth Resources 231
   Free Audio Programs Online, 231
   Free Video Programs Online, 231
   Free Webinars/Free Membership, 232
   People from this Book I Recommend Reading About,
   *   Studying, Getting to Know, 232*
   Planet Dan Folks Mentioned in this Book, 236
   Other Planet Dan Experts and Entrepreneurs
   *   You May Find Helpful, 238*
   Organizations Referenced in this Book, 240

About the Author 242
   Other Books by the Author, 243

   Index, 244
   The Most Incredible FREE Gift Ever, 250

Acknowledgments

This book owes an enormous debt, as do I, to Andrew Carnegie, Napoleon Hill, W. Clement Stone, Dr. Edward L. Kramer, Sidney Newton Bremer, and my personal friend and associate, Foster Hibbard.

Preface
How To Make Yourself Magnetic to Money

This is not a book about MAKING money.

This is not a book about CREATING wealth.

Both words, "making" and "creating," reinforce what I call the Work-Money Link, a limiting idea that we will change, a chain we will break in this book. Words like "MAKE" or "CREATE" suggest that you obtain wealth only through and in proportion to effort exerted. These words imply that wealth comes about primarily, if not only,z through hard work, through extreme exertion.

This book is about the *ATTRACTION* of wealth.

I use the word "attraction" most deliberately.

In this book, I hope to empower and equip you to attract all the wealth you want. With far greater ease than you've ever imagined. Faster than you think possible. With less work than you would think possible. In any economic conditions—booms or recessions—including the fast-emerging New Economy that I will speak about extensively in these pages.

This is a radical shift on several levels.

There is a philosophical component, so we will be discussing your thoughts and attitudes and beliefs about wealth. But we will not stop there. As an early mentor of mine said, you can't eat philosophy. There is a way of thinking that repels wealth, and that is, obviously, how most people think. There is a way to think that attracts wealth. If you think that way, you are magnetic to opportunity, money, and wealth. This is all-important, yet it is a hand often overplayed. A few years back, for example, there was an enormously popular made-for-DVD documentary promoting thought as the secret to wealth attraction, always an appealing promise, for obvious reasons, but a lie by omission. There's much more to it.

There is a strategic component. There are very practical things to do to put yourself in the right position, to set in motion the forces that attract wealth. I'm not talking about investing strategies; this is not a book about investing. You invest to create or preserve wealth. I'm talking about the attraction of wealth. So, relax, you need not fear yet another mind-numbing discussion of mutual funds and 401Ks and stocks and trends, illustrated with charts and graphs. Instead, we'll be dealing with entrepreneurial strategies, relationship strategies, influence strategies, and marketing strategies that, properly employed, make you magnetic to opportunity, money, and wealth. There are new mandates of The New Economy, too, requiring new strategies and clearer focus on time-honored ones. All will be discussed here.

Finally, there is a behavioral component. There are behaviors that repel wealth, and that is, obviously, how most people behave. There are ways to behave that attract wealth. If you behave that way, you are magnetic to opportunity, money, and wealth. Ultimately, it is my contention that wealth attraction is more about doing than thinking.

In total, this is all about making adjustments to the way you think and act, that make it easier to attract all the wealth you want, faster and easier than you can imagine.

WARNING!

Yes, a warning: when I say *radical* changes in beliefs and behavior, I mean it. A lot of what you are about to read is going to be very hard to swallow. You will be tempted to instantly reject it. You will find it contrary and challenging to what you've been taught and what you believe. It will make you uncomfortable. It's natural to simply turn off and move away from anything causing you discomfort. However, a great deal of discovery and growth and progress and success is preceded by discomfort.

This is a *very* blunt book—The "No B.S." in its title makes that promise. And a lot of what is published elsewhere about wealth is in the feel-good category. This book includes a fair amount of things those other authors probably know but keep to themselves, lacking the courage to say them publicly, certain they will offend people. I have never been concerned with who I may offend and I'm not about to start worrying about it now. I didn't even sugarcoat many of these discomfort producing statements, building up to them gently, wrapping them in entertaining parables. This IS the No B.S. truth about how entrepreneurs attract wealth, as I know it.

To avoid having wasted the price of this book and, more importantly, to avoid missing out on incredible opportunities to transform your life for the better, you need to tolerate some of this discomfort, to patiently and carefully consider ideas and suggestions that at first seem dead wrong, illogical, irrational, and unreasonable to you.

To encourage you, I'm going to briefly describe my "qualifications," to convince you that I am a person you should take seriously, even though I'm presenting ideas you find difficult to accept. I tell you these things not to brag. I have no need.

I started out in life broke, no family resources. I have no college degree. By traditional predictive factors, I'm a man least likely to succeed. Before age 50, solely via my own entrepreneurial pursuits, I had amassed sufficient wealth to allow me to stop working and never make another dollar if I so chose. I have built, bought, sold businesses, developed hugely successful businesses, even invented an entire industry. I have achieved prominence, some degree of fame. In recent years, money has flowed to me in ever increasing abundance even as my interest in it has waned. I have made millions of dollars a year in personal income. I own a nice home, own many racehorses, own other good investments, classic cars, have zero debt, and live exactly as I wish in every respect. I work closely, privately with hundreds of multi-millionaire and seven-figure-income entrepreneurs, most of whom have created their businesses from scratch, many quickly, many with my assistance from the start. These millionaires literally stand in line and pay huge sums for my advice. These people take me very seriously. I have taught them how to go beyond the making of money to the attraction of wealth.

This book, incidentally, is, in part, derived from a seminar I conducted only once, by my choice, attended by about a hundred entrepreneurs, each paying about $1,000.00 for the privilege. It is also based, in part, on discussions from a Wealth Attraction Coaching Group that I worked with, comprised of 18 entrepreneurs, most enjoying million and multi-million dollar annual incomes, each paying $14,000.00 to be in the group. My lowest consulting fee is currently $18,800.00 for a day, a substantially higher hourly rate than top lawyers and law firms or top doctors can command, and I'm pleased to say, there's usually a waiting list.

Again, I tell you all this to evidence the value and validity of the ideas in this book, even though they may seem "weird" to you.

If you stop to think about it, it's probably true that most of what you've been taught about money, opportunity, and wealth was taught to you by people without wealth. Most of what you've read or heard about wealth was said or written by the unwealthy. Most of the people you've associated with, whose opinions about money you've heard often, aren't wealthy. Most of what is your present Belief System about wealth was built with raw material you obtained from unwealthy sources.

In stark contrast to those sources, I am a wealthy source. If my ideas didn't contradict, conflict, and challenge those in your present belief system, something would be wrong!

Incidentally, I fully realize you may be quite successful in your own right. I suspect that's the case. Poor people rarely buy books with "wealth" in the title, just one of the many reasons they stay poor. So I do not discount your accomplishments or your knowledge. But I've worked with a great many successful people who struggled mightily to get there, who succeed despite their beliefs about wealth rather than thanks to them. I have watched such people go through the most amazing transformations and liberation with the ideas in this book. You will meet some of them in the book. No matter how successful you may be, I am confident you will find some ideas in this book that will surprise you, shock

How To Get a Collection of Wealth Attraction Tools—Free

I am eager for the ideas in this book to work for you, for you to put them to work for you. For that reason, I have assembled an entire "Wealth Attraction Tool Kit," which includes an "Action Guide" for this book, checklists, forms, Psychological Trigger Cards, a teleseminar, and an e-mail Course. To get your collection, you need to go online to www.NoBSBooks.com, to the section linked to this book. All these resources are free. Beyond that, there is also a free trial membership available that includes my newsletter, audio programs, webinars, and more—details on page 250 of this book. You can accept membership immediately.

you, challenge you, liberate you, benefit you. I am confident that Donald Trump could read this book and find something to use, to attract even greater wealth, more easily than ever before.

Ideally, our work on wealth attraction won't stop with this book.

Book Roadmap

Section 1 has 28 Wealth Magnets—including two that are entirely new to this otherwise revised and updated New Economy edition of this book originally published in 2006 and, I'm pleased to say, popular since then. These Magnets are not in sequential order because there is no sequential order to put them in. They are to be used simultaneously. You might think of them as puzzle pieces laid out on the tabletop, waiting for you to fit them together in a way that works best for you. You can also treat it as a cafeteria line, choosing and working with only the one or two or three that seem most important to you at the moment, but I would emphasize that the great wealth attractors use them all.

Section 2 provides two bonus chapters written by individuals who are applying many of the Magnets to their respective businesses in extraordinary ways.

Section 3, Wealth Resources, includes contact information or other references for interesting people mentioned throughout the book, a recommended reading list, and other support information. Here you will also find a FREE OFFER from me, so that you can experience the benefits of ongoing association as a Member of the Glazer-Kennedy Insider's Circle." You will also find instructions for accessing audio highlights of my live-recorded Wealth Attraction Seminar and my Renegade Millionaire System, which is online, on-demand, and also free of charge.

I recommend immediately taking advantage of your free Membership—there's no reason to wait until you've completed the book.

"Our brains become magnetized
with the dominating thoughts
which we hold in our minds, and,
by means with which no man is familiar,
these 'magnets' attract to us
the forces, the people,
the circumstances of life
which harmonize with the nature of
our dominating thoughts."

—NAPOLEON HILL,
AUTHOR OF *LAWS OF SUCCESS*,
THINK AND GROW RICH,
GROW RICH WITH PEACE OF MIND,
WWW.NAPOLEONHILLFOUNDATION.COM

WEALTH MAGNETS

Wealth Magnet 1
No Guilt

Most people's world view of wealth is as a zero-sum game. A big impediment to attraction of wealth is the idea that the amount of wealth floating around to be attracted is limited. If you believe it's limited, then you believe that each dollar you have came to you at someone else's expense, your gain another's loss. That makes your subconscious mind queasy. So it keeps your wealth attraction power turned down. Never to full power. To let it operate at full power would be unfair and harmful to others. If you are a decent human being, and you have this viewpoint, then you will always modulate your wealth attraction power. If too much starts pouring in too easily, guilt is produced as if it were insulin being produced by the pancreas after pigging out on a whole pizza. You can't help it. Your wealth magnetism will be turned down *for you*.

Think about the words *"fair share."*

They are powerful, dangerous words.

As an ethical, moral person, you probably think—*"hey, I don't want more than my fair share."* But that reveals belief that wealth is limited. If you believe wealth is unlimited, there's no such thing as a share of it. Everybody's share is unlimited. There's nothing to have a share of. There's only unlimited. Your fair share is all you can possibly attract. As is anybody and everybody else's.

In business, there's a similar idea: market share. But again that presumes a finite, limited market, instead of an infinitely expandable market.

In the New Economy, market share is one of the most antiquated of concepts. Boundaries are broken—even the smallest of businesses can be global in reach, thanks largely to the internet. Consumers have access to a multiplied and multiplying range of choices, so classic brand loyalty has been replaced by search for and expectation of the thing that is precisely, perfectly appropriate. The market for all manner of goods and services is greater than ever before yet the fragmentation of the market itself is greater and more complex than ever before. The attraction of wealth in this environment has little to do with somehow "locking up" a limited portion of a limited market and everything to do with directly connecting with individuals and meeting their needs and interests. When you think in terms of being in the business of creatively meeting the needs and interests of individuals, it's obvious that the size of the market available to you is limited only by your own creativity and initiative. Further, that whatever connection you create and accomplish has no relationship to what anyone else does, whether a lot or a little. Clinging to old ideas of limitation blocks access to new opportunity!

A Tale of Two Teenagers

Imagine being a teenager in a family in severe financial trouble. Money is very scarce. There's you, two brothers, father and mother. When everybody sits down to dinner and Mom puts the food on the table, you know that's all the food there is. The bowl of mashed potatoes is all the mashed potatoes there are. You are hungry. You really want a big second helping of mashed potatoes. The bowl is right in front of you, within easy reach. But instead of just reaching out, dragging it over, and scooping out a pile of potatoes, you stop to look around and see who has potatoes on their plate. You look to see if your father's had plenty of potatoes. You hold back from fulfilling your desire out of concern that others may not yet have had their fair share, may be hungrier than you. You do not want someone else going hungry as a result of your appetite.

I don't have to imagine that. I lived it.

Now imagine being a teenager in a family living an abundant life, with great prosperity. When Mom puts dinner on the table, you know there's plenty more where it came from. The refrigerator's full of food. So are the cupboards. There are always leftovers after dinner. You are hungry. You really want a big second helping of mashed potatoes. The bowl is right in front of you, within easy reach. Without a second thought, you reach out, drag the bowl over, and scoop out all the potatoes you want.

In these examples, of course, you're acting consciously. In the first case, in the financially troubled family, you consciously hold back, sacrifice, do not take what is right in front of you for the taking.

Similarly but subconsciously, if you believe, at all, on any level, that wealth is limited, that there's *not* plenty to go around, you will hold back, you won't take everything that's right in front of you. Your emotions about wealth will be cautious, measured, restricted, suppressed, timid.

If you can make every last smidgen of belief that wealth is limited go away, your attraction of wealth will suddenly, automatically, go from modulated, limited, and suppressed to full power, and opportunity, money, and wealth will quickly flow to

*"I've called the family together to announce that, because of inflation,
I'm going to have to let two of you go."*

you in greater quantities and at greater speed than you've ever before experienced.

People get ingrained in their heads that money taken from Person A and moved to Person B enriches Person B at the expense of Person A. Certainly, the liberal politicians either believe it or pander to it, one or the other. Some religious doctrines and religious leaders posit this idea. There are lots of ways this belief might be firmly planted in your head; maybe even in elementary school math class. If Johnny has 4 pieces of candy and gives 2 of them to Jim, how many does Johnny have left? The answer needed to ace the quiz is 2. But the "problem" ignores the fact that Johnny can simply open his hand and have as many pieces of candy appear in it as he'd like. After all, there's no global shortage of candy. When you actually understand wealth, you know that Johnny can have 4 pieces, give Jim 2 pieces, but then have 42 pieces.

What's even weirder and tougher for math teachers is that Johnny is much more likely to have 42 if he does give away 2 of the 4 than if he hoards the 4. But that's another topic for a different place in this book. For now, let's keep it simple:

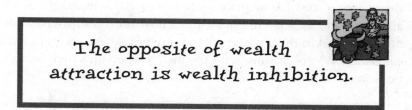

The opposite of wealth attraction is wealth inhibition.

Most people are so wealth-inhibited they never even think in terms of getting wealthy. Their thoughts on this subject are limited to buying a lottery ticket or fantasizing about some unknown, long-lost uncle leaving them a fortune in his will. But there are a lot of people who do, at some point, start seriously trying to figure out how they might convert their knowledge, ability, time, energy, and effort into real wealth. You may be in that group—it may be the reason you were attracted to and purchased this book. So, a warning: the majority of people in this group never get traction, never get going, never get wealthy because they suffer from wealth inhibition.

If you believe wealth is limited, if you view it as a zero-sum game, you are inhibited. This inhibition affects all sorts of things you do or don't do, such as what you'll charge, for example, or who you'll ask for money.

I've spent a lot of time working with people in sales. Those who identify themselves as salespeople, like folks selling insurance, cars, fire alarms, as well as those who don't identify themselves as salespeople but are, like dentists and psychologists. Two things are true for all of them that reflect wealth inhibition.

One has to do with price. Most fear discussion of price, fear-raising prices, are paranoid about pricing higher than their competitors. I have had to work long and hard to get some people to raise their prices or fees far beyond present levels, industry norms, or competitors' prices, in order to charge what their service and expertise is really worth to their clientele. In numerous cases, I've forced fee or price increases of 200% to 2,000% with absolutely no adverse impact—that's how far underpriced a lot of people are! In these situations, we are not dealing with practical issues. We are dealing with the businessperson's own inhibitions and fears.

> Because this is such an important subject that can lead to such huge breakthroughs in a business, I developed an entire seminar on the subject of PRICE ELASTICITY, which you can take as an online course. Get details at www.DanKennedy.com.

Second is pulling the punch when closing the sale. I sometimes joke about one of my own businesses—freelance advertising copywriting—where I routinely charge fees of $100,000.00 to $150,000.00 or more for a complete project, no less than $25,000.00 for a single ad or sales letter. Plus royalties. I say that the primary requirement for getting such fees has little to do with my prowess as a copywriter and everything to do with my ability to keep a straight face and voice free of stammer when quoting the fee! This may be the reason a lot of art and antique dealers write the price down on a piece of stationery and slide it across the desk to you. There's truth in the joke. When the dentist quotes his $70,000.00 case to the patient, when the private residence club quotes the $215,000.00 membership fee, when anyone speaks any price or fee, there is the tendency for tremors, the temptation to discount without ever even being asked, out of fear, inhibition, and presumption. In short, to pull the punch.

Consider the salesman who goes into a person's home to sell fire alarms. (I have a corporate client in this industry.) The fire alarm salesman with the stuffed Dalmatian under his arm and the burning house DVD marches in and discovers that he is in a place of relative poverty—at least by his standards. The two kids are on a thread-bare carpet in the living room. They probably have a good television, but pretty much everything else in the house is obviously hand-me-down, beat-up, falling apart, springs sticking up out of the couch seat. He can clearly see that these people aren't doing well. Conversationally, he discovers Papa hasn't worked in four months and one of the kid's got some kind of problem that causes big medical bills, and on and on and on. The salesperson becomes increasingly queasy about closing these people on the $2,000.00 fire alarm sale. And, in many cases, he will not close the sale. He will subconsciously pull his punches, accept the first objection easily. Or he'll consciously, deliberately throw the game at the end, toss that one aside, and get out of there.

This is an analogy to the way everybody behaves in all sorts of situations, if operating from a belief of limited wealth.

My friend Glenn Turner tells the story from his earliest selling days of actually being chased by somebody who was mad that he wouldn't sell him a sewing machine. Glenn thought the person couldn't afford it, shouldn't go into debt to buy it, and obviously cut his presentation short and abruptly got up and left—only to be literally chased down the street and caught by the husband, who called him on not trying to make the sale. "How dare you think for me? I've got a right to buy that thing for my wife if I want to."

My speaking colleague Zig Ziglar has a similar story from his earliest days selling cookware, about the customer that was saving up the money to put in indoor plumbing. Discovering that they didn't even have indoor plumbing, Zig backed off and didn't try to close the sale on the cookware. And the people were annoyed, they really wanted the pots and pans. The husband said: We can put the plumbing in later. Mamma wants those pots now.

The queasiness about price, about whom somebody is selling to, about their ability to pay, their ability to afford it is all deadly. And the truth is, anytime you start to make those decisions for other people, it really reflects more about what's going on internally with you than it does with anything else.

Oh, and by the way, if you were that fire alarm salesman who deliberately threw the sale, how would you feel about not exerting your best efforts if you turned on the TV news the next night and saw that family's house burned to the ground and they had died in the fire? Oops.

There's something else to get clear about the people who are without money, that you perceive to be disadvantaged for one reason or another and you question whether you should sell something regardless of whether you get any of their money or not—they're going to be without money next week, too.

The reason they're without money has absolutely nothing whatsoever to do with your existence, what you sell or fail to sell, nor does it have to do with the way money works in the real world. It has to do with them. And whether you take it, somebody else takes it, the liquor store takes it, the church takes it, whoever takes it, I promise you somebody's getting it. Because if they're without money now, they're going to be without money again. And most of them are going to be without money permanently, because they never gain or act on an understanding of how money works.

I know that sounds harsh. And you may not be a face-to-face salesperson and never need to sit across a desk or table from someone you think "can't afford it" and sell to them anyway. But the truth about this particular situation is the bigger truth about the entire world of money and wealth. That truth is, whatever amount you get has nothing to do with how much or how little anyone else has. Ever.

If you want your wealth attraction glowing and functioning at full power, you can't have *any* queasiness. You can't have *any* reluctance. You can't have *any* inhibition. You can't *ever* pull a punch. In the bigger sense, you have to understand that whatever financial position anyone you know is in, anyone you do business with is in, anyone, period, is in, has nothing to do with you. In the biggest sense, you have to understand that whatever the state of economic affairs in the world, it has nothing to do with how much wealth you accumulate. **Your wealth is addition for you but subtraction for no one.**

Unless and until you buy this premise hook, line, and sinker, you will always suffer from wealth inhibition.

One of the many great masters of wealth attraction worthy of your study is Gene Simmons, creator of the rock band, KISS. In recent years, you may have seen Gene in the reality-TV show about his life on A&E, *Gene Simmons Family Jewels*. We had Gene as a guest speaker at one of the conferences we hold each year for our Glazer-Kennedy Insider's Circle™ Members got to hear his life story and entrepreneurial strategies firsthand, and I spent a fair amount of private time offstage, kibitzing with him. I routinely recommend his book, *Sex, Money, Kiss* as a good, candid look into the way a made-from-scratch, multi-millionaire entrepreneur adept at wealth attraction thinks about money. You may be offended or shocked, but you'll learn a lot from Gene. (To be invited to our conferences, you need only accept the complimentary membership offered on page 250.)

"Be clear, be truthful.

Stand there proudly,

unapologetically,

unabashedly, and say,

'I love cash.

It will get me

everything

I want in life.' "

—GENE SIMMONS

Newman's Own

No one mentioned this when reporting on the death, life, and work of Paul Newman. Much was made of his extraordinary acting career, including, I think, accurate observation that there was much more depth in some of his later roles than in his early, more popular performances. If you never saw *The Verdict*, rent it. A little bit was said about his auto racing investments and activities including his own somewhat improbable, late in life driving—a clue to his competitiveness. More was said about his liberal politics and protest; he was proud of being on President Nixon's enemies list. And he was a liberal even we conservatives could admire and respect, because he was knowledgable and informed, principled, consistent, and walked his talk. Most was said about his development of his famous food company, which donates its profits to charity. But no one said anything about this, in Newman's Own Words:

> *"Now that I'm heavily into peddling food, I begin to understand the romance of business, the allure of being the biggest fish in the pond and the juice you get from* ***beating out your competitors.***"

He also said that he could not "lay claim to some terribly philanthropic instinct—it was a combination of circumstances." Had the business stayed small, as the lark it was to start, he says it would never have gone charitable. Of course, it quickly grew big, and hundreds of millions of dollars of the Newman's Own brand products have been sold, and the charitable support provided will now continue long after his death, a fine legacy. Somewhat accidentally, the business Paul Newman created and lent his celebrity to has become a new model for many for-profit companies with the purpose of funding social causes or supporting charitable activities.

But my main point here is that behind the legendary blue eyes lived a *ferocious competitor.* In his acting career, in his racing, in his business, Newman derived immense pleasure from beating out his competitors. A truth not often included in highly successful entrepreneurs' press kits and autobiographies, but that is revealed in interviews and others' profiles of them, is that they are not *nice.* They are tough. In specific competitive situations, they are even ruthless. They play to win and are not usually "good losers." I listen to people and watch people closely, to try and determine the extent and depth and constancy of their competitive drive—or lack thereof. Personally, every single day that I choose to work, I compete. I compete with the clock; I compete against the odds, to develop successful marketing campaigns; I compete in the cluttered, crowded marketplace for attention. When I was a speaker at events with a number of other speakers who also sold from the platform, I always wanted to hit my targets but also beat all others' dollars per head, and connived to get that information so I could tell whether I won or lost. It's my observation that winners have an emotional need to win, find a way to score themselves in everything they do, and rarely shrug off losing, however that may be defined. If you intently, thoroughly study any famously successful entrepreneur present or past about whom a wealth of information is available, you'll make that same observation.

Wealth Magnet 2
Unequivocal Belief In Abundance

Water, water everywhere but not a drop to drink. Our world is no desert island. There's money, money everywhere. Drink all you want.

If you do not hang out with people who own private planes or shares in private jets, or at least fly first class everywhere they go . . . if you do not hang out with people who have their shirts and suits custom tailored . . . if you do not hang out with people who own racehorses or boats or vacation homes . . . if you do not hang out with people who are extremely prosperous and adept at wealth attraction, you might be fooled into thinking that money is "tight" or in limited supply or hard to come by. And based on those thoughts, you might inhibit your own wealth attraction. Or you might think such people are rare, in small number. They are not.

While it is true that the recession, stock market collapse, real estate value reversals, and related economic trauma of past, recent years did take its toll on the super-rich, the merely rich, and the mass-affluent or nearly rich, it's also true that it left plenty of people in these populations, with plenty more moving up as we speak. After all, if you are worth $100-million or $10-million and temporarily see 10%, 20%, or even 30% of your net worth disappear, you are still worth $70-million, $80-million, or $90-million, or if starting with $10-million, still worth $7-million, $8-million, or $9-million. The loss is annoying, possibly scary, briefly. But it doesn't change the fact that you are wealthy. Further, one thing about everybody who has amassed most or all of their wealth through their own ingenuity, effort, investment, and attraction (as opposed to inheritance, hitting the lottery, or having been president of the United States and then cashing in afterward) is that they know how to replace wealth lost; they know how to attract it, and are quite confident of their ability to do so.

It happens that I travel by private jet myself, and I can tell you there was, recently, a downturn in all aspects of the private aviation business. But I can also tell you that there are still waiting lines to land at and take off from private terminals at many airports, multi-million dollar jets being purchased every day, and companies like NetJets ferrying about more self-made affluents you've never heard of than celebrities you have heard of, to and from their second and third homes, weekend golf games, vacations, and, of course, business meetings.

The rising tide of affluence is so great we even added a newsletter to our stable, which I edit, devoted entirely to marketing to the affluent, and wrote an entire book on the subject, *The No B.S. Guide to Marketing to the Affluent*.

Anyway, if these are not the circles you hang out in, then poking your nose in there will be very good for you. Exposure to the reality of a world you may only think of as fodder for TV and

Be Where the Money Is!

I edit a special newsletter entirely devoted to the subject of marketing to the affluent and mass affluent, the *No B.S. Marketing to the Affluent Letter*. Information at www.DanKennedy.com. There is also a book on the subject in this series, *No B.S. Guide to Marketing to the Affluent*.

movies and a few glossy magazines can alter your entire attitude about attracting wealth for yourself. The very idea of personal wealth attraction is easier to accept the more you personally see, experience, and understand just how much free-flowing wealth there is to attract. It's a bit like never actually seeing the ocean from a penthouse balcony and only reading about it in a book or seeing pictures in a magazine—the enormity of it, the vastness of it just doesn't hit you until you experience it in person.

I suggest the following experiences: visit The Forum Shops in Las Vegas, Rodeo Drive in Beverly Hills, or Bergdorf Goodman in New York City. Vacation in Boca Raton, Florida, Scottsdale, Arizona, or Aspen, Colorado. Immediately go to your nearest bookstore and pick up copies of *The Robb Report, Millionaire, Worth,* and *Town & Country* magazines. Go on a field trip to a classic car auction or a racehorse auction. In short, in person and at a distance through media, immerse yourself in the lifestyles of the affluent. Not only will you be surprised at the prices cheerfully paid for goods and services, you'll be more amazed at the vast array of very high-priced goods and services designed for affluent consumers—you'll be even more amazed at just how many affluent consumers there are.

The more aware you make your own mind—conscious and subconscious—of just how much affluence there is, just how

"I was at my sister's today. They have two pots."

much money is moving around, the more easily you will attract wealth. So this is no idle exercise I suggest. It is an important step in conditioning your mind to attract wealth. And, just as your body must be conditioned for health and fitness and longevity, your mind must be conditioned for wealth. This observing of money flowing around the affluent is such an important and beneficial exercise, I have taken one of my Wealth Attraction Coaching Groups to Disney's Animal Kingdom Lodge on a "field trip," all staying on the concierge floor, taking the Sunrise Safari, lunching with a staff Imagineer, eating in the five-star restaurants. I took my Coaching Groups on a field trip to The Forum Shops. I give subscriptions to *The Robb Report* as client gifts. Even if you are not yet living an affluent lifestyle, you must immerse yourself in expanded awareness of what it is like and how many people are.

To believe the streets are awash with money, you need to see streets awash with money. If there aren't any in your own neighborhood, you just need to get out more!

Neiman-Marcus invented the idea of offering extraordinarily expensive, unique items in their annual holiday catalogs years ago—initially, more as a means of getting publicity than making spectacularly profitable sales. However, over years the practice has led to Neiman-Marcus and many other catalog merchants inventing unusual gift offers. Several years ago, Victoria's Secret offered a diamond encrusted bra for a million dollars. One of my favorites was presented in a catalog called *Gentleman's Domain*: a product from the Eli Bridge Company, a manufacturer that builds amusement park rides, has been building them for the industry for 100 years. With the offer in *Gentleman's Domain*, for a mere $300,000.00 you could have the real thing in your backyard, a 67-foot-high, 16-seat Ferris wheel. The catalog copy warned that you'd need a 220-volt power outlet. And since it weighed almost 20 tons, you may have wanted to have the patio checked out before getting started.

There are two lessons here. One, another illustration of the amount of money flowing, and two, the opportunity to dip into the flowing stream as you wish, given enough ingenuity to create something captivating to people. While these kind of outrageous gift examples date back to 1955, when Neiman-Marcus began the creative exercise in response to the blossoming of the new oil-rich in Texas, it is a terrific success clue for The New Economy in which everybody expects something unique, of particular and precise relevance to them, and is willing to pay premium prices or fees for it. (In Neiman-Marcus's Christmas catalogs: a jewel-encrusted tiger, a $588,000.00 stocked and staffed Noah's Ark, and his-and-her jets.)

Of course, most people's reaction to an outrageous example like this is to cry "irrelevant!" After all, your customers don't have this kind of money to blow, your customers are tight-fisted cheapskates, you have a hard time selling to your customers, yada yada. Pfui. A few years back, I produced an infomercial-style video brochure for a client who builds top-of-the-line, expensive backyard sheds. Not the tin jobs you think of. These are more like miniature houses, with peaked roofs, doors, windows, flower boxes, and complete interiors, with workbenches, bookshelves, and cabinetry. The priciest of them could even be sold in the Neiman-Marcus catalog! To shoot the video, I took a crew to a number of the customers' backyards, to see their sheds and tape their testimonial comments.

One happy couple with not one but two sheds in their backyard, his-and-hers sheds, are both retired and on Social Security, and he's got one small pension. They're totally on a fixed income. *Two* sheds.

Another guy with the biggest shed and a big pond in his backyard started out telling me something of a sob story. If you heard it, you'd assume he didn't have two nickels to rub together. But somehow, miraculously, he dug up about $20,000.00 for landscaping and a koi pond, and another $10,000.00 for the shed.

The truth, known to all smart marketers is: Everybody somehow finds plenty of money to buy whatever they decide they want to buy. There's always a lot of "hidden money" in the market as a whole and in the vast majority of households and businesses. It hides from everyone failing to offer sufficiently motivating and interesting offers. It is invisible to entrepreneurs with vision blocked by their own ideas about the absence of available spending power.

Lots of people complain about how tough they have it, raising a family, three kids, both parents having to work. Both parents and all three kids have cellphones; about $90.00 a month in charges. Both of the older kids are in not one but several activities: dance, karate, Little League. Both parents drive new autos. There's a satellite dish on the side of the house, a big flat-screen TV in the den, a TV in every bedroom. They wouldn't know "tough" if it bit 'em in the butt, and they freely buy whatever they decide to buy.

It is a huge, huge, huge mistake for you to accept any part of the suggestion that money's tight, hard to get, that your customers don't have money or won't spend it. And if by some freak, rare, incredible chance you actually have managed to put yourself into a position where the people you are doing business with are short of money or are tight about spending it, bubba, you choose your customers. Switch to some who freely spend. There are plenty of them out there. One of the keys to turning your wealth attraction power on to max is acceptance of all the responsibility for your outcomes in life. The nature of your customers, the responsiveness of your customers, the buying behavior of your customers in their relationship with you is your responsibility—not theirs and not anybody else's.

Don't Buy What the Bad Newsmongers Are Selling

Beware the news media. For some perverse reasons of their own, about which I have my suspicions, the mainstream media constantly under-reports good economic news and over-hypes bad economic news. During the recent recession, the media loved to compare it to The Great Depression, to such an egregious extent that my friends at the prestigious Business And Media Institute at Media Research Center issued an entire, detailed report for the media, the public, and groups like my clients, de-bunking the comparison. It is a huge, huge, huge mistake for you to accept the mainstream media's biased, liberal agenda-driven misrepresentation of the state of the economy or of the amount and level of opportunity in this country—at any time. And whatever you do, do NOT listen to any of the even more outrageously inaccurate assertions from Michael Moore and his ilk. There is a contingent of Moore-types who insist on promoting the idea that there is a teeny, tiny group of evil rich versus a gigantic population of viciously oppressed masses for whom there is no opportunity. The spew of Moore, and others who echo it, is toxic. I have written a lengthy article about this, originally intended for the *No B.S. Business Success* book, omitted through editorial decisions, and subsequently published in my autobiography, *Unfinished Business*, which you can find information about at www.renegademillionaire.com.

Visit BusinessAndMedia.org for research-based analysis of media reporting on business, financial, and political issues. BMI publishes my political column and numerous other leading columnists and thought-leaders, and posts new information and commentary daily.

The truth is that the biggest, fastest-growing, most expansive and expanding segment of the American population is mass affluent, not poor. Admittedly, this trend was temporarily slowed by recession, but demographics guarantee that it will pick up steam and hit a faster stride than ever before, post-recession, in The New Economy.

Here's something interesting about affluence. I was born in 1954. Owning the color TV in the neighborhood was a sign of affluence. When I was a kid, we were the only people in our entire neighborhood near Cleveland, Ohio, to have a swimming pool. That was a big deal. Getting a new car, a big deal. In the 70s, the two-car household was affluent. Now it's a two-home household. A few years back, when I was still flying commercial, on a flight from Cleveland to Orlando, I realized through conversation that every single person in the first class seats owned a home in Cleveland and another home in Florida. There is, right now, this minute, more disposable income by any measurement—dollars, percentages, ratios, you pick the statistics you like—than ever before. There are more people invested in real estate in addition to their homes and in the stock market than ever, and despite stalls and reverse in values and value growth of these assets, there are more millionaires than ever before. The biggest wealth transfer in American history from my parents' generation to mine is in progress, with another to follow, from my generation to the next.

On top of that, new categories of products and services, new entertainments and recreations, new industries, new opportunities abound. Stop and think about all the businesses that didn't even exist when you were a kid. I marvel at it all.

It seems that every day, somebody invents another new means of attracting wealth. Consider the simple but fast-growing homebased business of mommy-blogging. If you've never heard of it, it's nearly nine years old, and expanding exponentially. A growing list of major corporations have moved from merely giving free product samples to paying sponsorship fees, per-posting fees, and ad dollars to stay-at-home mommies who use and write about their products on their blogs, giving mom-to-mom recommendations. Most of these bloggers are small-time operators, picking up free products, a few hundred dollars a month, maybe an all-expense paid junket now and again, like a family trip to Sea World. But an increasing number are moving up to thousands of dollars in monthly income, some even more. There are even aggregators, organizing these fragmented solo operators into groups, under single umbrellas, so bigger dollars can be secured from advertisers. The activity has become so significant that, in mid-2009, the Federal Trade Commission began discussions about regulating it as advertising media and imposing requirements for disclosures about payments received by the bloggers. This grass-roots, made-by-moms activity is likely to morph into an organized, substantial industry generating hundreds of millions of dollars a year and, yes, creating wealth for many involved—as well as for up-and-coming businesses that find ways to use this unusual advertising and marketing media. This is but one of literally thousands of examples of new wealth-creation devices and opportunities springing to life all around you.

I am absolutely convinced that if you don't do well financially in America today, it is either due to utter ignorance of opportunity or choice. It definitely is NOT due to lack of opportunity. You need to be convinced of this, too.

These fact-based beliefs are essential to turning off wealth inhibition and turning up wealth attraction. If you do not share these beliefs, if you doubt and question the fact of unlimited, readily available abundance of both opportunity and money, then you need to invest time and energy on your own fact-finding research mission and make this sale to yourself. Otherwise, to borrow from a past friend, the late Jim Newman, author of the fine book *Release Your Brakes*, you are driving down the highway to wealth, one foot on the gas but the other foot riding the brake.

The Day That Changed a Doctor's Money Awareness Forever

Let me tell you about a Critical Day In My Life.

I was making small talk with a female patient, Sally R., who constantly fought me on receiving care, complained about what her insurance covered and didn't cover, and told me she just couldn't afford "all these adjustments"—even though she felt better with them, felt worse without them. This fateful Monday, Sally casually mentioned, "Could you be a little careful today? Saturday I had a deep tissue massage and I'm a bit sore still, mostly in my neck."

I was stunned. As if a bucket of ice water had been thrown in my face.

But I stayed calm and in the same casual tone as hers, asked where she'd received the massage. And she told me—in glowing terms—of going to the new, fancy spa on Columbus Avenue. "My husband's partner's wife told me to go there to get a great facial. By the way, I don't think you've ever met my husband. He and his partner own the big law firm across from the courthouse downtown, the one with the clock on the building's tower. Anyway, when I went to the spa for my first appointment, they asked me if I had any other issues . . . . I told them I come here to have my back cracked . . . and they suggested I sign up for a package of deep tissue massages that would compliment the adjustments and help me feel better longer."

I was angry. Felt betrayed. Sally'd been poor-mouthing me to the point I'd reduced her per visit charges, and agreed to send her a bill at the end of each month rather than having her pay per-visit. Now I knew she was paying big prices—CASH—at a fancy spa. And was married to a prominent attorney. (I later got over being angry at her and rightfully got good and mad AT ME.)

When Sally left, she even put off making her next appointments because "it's just so expensive and I don't want to run up too big a bill. I'll call you if I start feeling badly. Thanks, Dr. Johnson."

Thanks Dr. Johnson, indeed.

This was a Critical Day In My Life. I sat down and thought about what had just happened—and how it was certainly a "dirty little secret" among many of my other patients, and other chiropractors' patients from coast to coast. Maybe you've heard the author and speaker Jim Rohn talk about "the day that turned his life around." This was such a day for me. It *liberated* me, from being slave to what I thought others could or would pay, and *emboldened* me to charge what I was worth—and work for no less.

—Dr. Michael Johnson, D.C.

Dr. Johnson operates a thriving, successful, multi-therapy clinic with emphasis on treating patients with chronic pain conditions in Appleton, Wisconsin. He also provides consulting and business coaching on "The Johnson Methods" for innovative treatment, practice development, and practice management to thousands of chiropractic physicians nationwide. Contact him at www.txchronicpain.com, www.askdr-johnson.com, or 1-800-846-8438.

Wealth Magnet 3
Break Free of "Fairness"

A lot of the authors, speakers, and teachers of "prosperity" in the metaphysical community are far from prosperous themselves. Over the years, quite a few have privately confessed their lack of financial success to me, and expressed puzzlement over it. Typically, the conversation has to do with their idea of "justice." They believe that because they do "good work" they deserve to be wealthy and that wealth should occur. There are also a lot of these people who perpetually beat themselves up, with the idea that their lack of financial success is about them somehow not deserving it, so they need to work on themselves, to be a more deserving person. While *a sense of* deserving is critically important to wealth attraction, there's a much bigger mental and emotional block stopping the flow of wealth to many.

One of the leading companies teaching negotiation skills to corporate executives, Charles Karrass's company, has had this as its slogan for many years:

> "You don't get what you deserve.
> You get what you negotiate."

The metaphysical opposite of this is: "I'm just not using the mental principles well enough. If I just think more positively, [keyword: just] things will turn around."

If you compare the two ideas, you'll see that the metaphysical version puts the responsibility for what will happen "out there." *Things* will turn around. Not that *you* will turn things around. It's a difference between passive and active. The statement about negotiation puts the responsibility for outcomes on you. And it acknowledges a very important fact: The marketplace does not function on fairness. If that were true, top talent would always win out; we know it does not. The safest wager in the world is that, somewhere, there are starving artists with infinitely more talent than Thomas Kincade or Robert Wyland. Doubt it? Ask any starving artists about Kincade! Somewhere, there are starving writers with infinitely more talent than James Patterson or Stephen King. During the nine years that I was one of only two fixtures on the biggest, most successful public seminar tour in America, visiting 25 to 27 cities a year, drawing 10,000 to 35,000 people to each event, and being paid over a million dollars a year, countless professional speakers struggling just to pay their bills puzzled aloud, to others behind my back, some to my face, how this could be—clearly I was not as "good" a speaker as they were or as many others were. And I cheerfully acknowledged they were right about that. I have never been insulted by it. I have sometimes been sympathetic, sometimes amused with their befuddlement and frustration. They just couldn't grasp that money does not move from one place or person to another simply and purely because of fairness. Talent can attract wealth, but superior talent alone very rarely does. Instead, there is a combination of magnetic forces put to work by those who most successfully attract wealth, notably those described in this book. Responsibility is a very powerful wealth attractant.

To rewrite the Karrass statement, I would say: You don't get what you (inherently) deserve. You get what you deliberately and intentionally attract not only by who you are but also by what you think, say, do, and get others to do. By the situations, circumstances, contacts, relationships, and opportunities you engineer.

Being an exceptionally talented person alone is not sufficient. Being a moral, spiritual, "good," deserving person alone is just not sufficient. In a purely fair marketplace, it might be. But it isn't. In many ways, The New Economy is even harsher in its rejection of those who feel entitled by virtue or talent or some similar attribute, because consumers have so many more choices in every category, so much more media vying for their attention, so much more competition by creative, aggressive, determined, and persistent entrepreneurs and marketers who do accept full and complete responsibility for their outcomes. On the other hand, The New Economy offers greater opportunity than ever for those who "get it."

Ultimately, as always, the way the majority thinks about money is wrong. Thinking that virtue or talent or superior product quality or service entitles you to success is fantastical and foolish.

An extension of this sort of thinking is the surprisingly popular argument that the 9/11 attack was our fault, in whole or part, because we have so much and other countries have so little and because we have an immoral society. Our collective ability to attract wealth somehow justifies others' evil toward us. So if we were just more moral and more generous, we wouldn't deserve what happened to us on 9/11 and it never would have happened. Therefore, we should close the Defense Department and take all that money and divide it up between the less-fortunate people in all these other countries, and we should spend it on churches and moral education in this country, and we wouldn't need a Defense Department. If we're just "better people," we'll be more deserving of peace and tranquility and security, and we'll have it. This idea is championed by fools. If you want to philosophically fantasize that this is the way the world should work, that's fine. But don't suggest it's the way the world does work.

> "Rules such as 'if I hold positive thoughts about prosperity, money will just start pouring into my life' are just too simplistic to work . . . money exists in the physical domain. Money doesn't come as the result of thoughts in the metaphysical realm; it comes **as the result of actions** in the physical domain."
>
> —MARIA NEMETH, PH.D., AUTHOR OF
> THE ENERGY OF MONEY, WWW.YOUANDMONEY.COM

Money has no moral conscience. It finds its way into the hands of pornographers just as it does Bible publishers. And I mean no disrespect to either. Trying to impose your opinions of "good" and "bad," "moral" and "immoral," "deserving" and "undeserving" onto money is even more futile than trying to impose them on people.

Money moves based on non-judgmental market forces, not morality. The difficult truth is: Being a good person, being a better person, being an exceptionally talented person, making or selling the better or even best product, or delivering the finest service does not automatically entitle you to wealth nor does it do anything to directly strengthen your wealth attraction. If you think that you should be financially rewarded because you are honest, hard-working, and kind to old people and pets, you're in for a very disappointing life. If you think God should intervene with the lotto on your behalf because you volunteer at the soup kitchen, you'll wind up disliking God. And clinging to these Pollyannaish, erroneous beliefs stands in the way of wealth moving to you.

If you want to easily attract a lot of money, you have to come to grips with what money is and isn't, the very nature of money, the energy of money, and how money moves about from one home to another.

Money doesn't have a conscience. It's paper. That's all it is. It's just paper. It's not significantly different than the paper that's in your book. It's green and it's got some kind of woven crap in it so that, theoretically, we can't counterfeit it. But it's paper. It doesn't know if you're a priest or a pornographer. Look, it's paper. That's all it is. Nothing less. It's just paper. It doesn't have a conscience, it doesn't know what you are, doesn't know what you do, doesn't care. It just moves around. That's all.

If money or the movement of money functioned on conscience, there never could be a Bernie Madoff, not even for a week let alone two decades. There couldn't have been a Jessie James or a John Dillinger. The money would stop before it got to them. It would put on the brakes. It would speak. It would say, "Wait a minute! You're doing something we don't approve of. We're not coming into your hands." The stuff would work like Matrix movie stuff. "Stop! Go back!" And you wouldn't be able to get it. But it doesn't do that.

Money has its own, different definition of "fairness." It moves to those who do the things that are magnetic to it. If you put a powerful magnet on the tool bench of a good man or a tool

I was recently reviewing a transcript of Jim Rohn's speech from a Glazer-Kennedy Insider's Circle™ SuperConference and caught the most concise explanation yet of why so many people go through life disappointed about money, envious and resentful of others' prosperity, mystified by others they view of lesser credentials or ability doing so much better than they are; and why all liberal or socialist redistribution of wealth fails so miserably. Rohn said, "Money does not go to need." A lot of people think it should, and that's why they are so frustrated. Money does not accept your ideas of its moral responsibility or of justice, and cannot be governed by them. So it is not attracted by or to need. The fact that you need more customers, sales, or profits to meet payroll or stay in business or send your kids to college or retire is of no interest to money, is unattractive to money, on many levels, even repellant to it. Anyone who focuses on their need attracts more need. Every attempt to force money to go and live with the needy fails; the money crawls out the window in dark of night and escapes.

The late JIM ROHN is one of the most celebrated personal development thought-leaders of our time. Visit www.JimRohn.com.

bench of a bad man, metal filings will still be drawn across the bench to the magnet. That's its fairness: simple, basic, *primal* cause and effect.

That doesn't mean you should be a pornographer. I'm not suggesting that. It doesn't mean you should run a Ponzi scheme. I'm not suggesting that. In fact, there are very pragmatic arguments for honesty and integrity, and choosing to produce and market products and services that enrich and improve peoples' lives, and for developing whatever talent you may have and whatever skills you can acquire to their highest and best levels. What I'm suggesting is you've got to get out of your head that by not doing "bad" things and by doing things that are "good," that alone attracts and multiplies. It doesn't. It may make your next life a better deal. You may be in a cool place instead of a warm place. You may not come back as a toad. Whatever your belief system is about afterlife, it may have impact there. But here and now, there are cause-and-effect principles of wealth attraction completely separated from virtue.

Forget the entire idea of *entitlement*. Focus on *engineering*—on engineering a situation for yourself that weaves together all the magnetic forces that influence the movement of money and puts them to work on your behalf.

Wealth Magnet 4
Accepting Your Role and Responsibilities

O h, you're an entrepreneur? Greedy bastard! Surely you know that's what some people think about you, say about you behind your back.

A successful entrepreneur drives down the street in his Rolls-Royce or builds his mansion. If not to his face, behind his back, many grumble about his greed. But if they hit the mega-millions lottery they might very well do the same things—most lottery winners do. It's not a moral objection to greed they're expressing. It's the sin of envy.

Too often, achievement, accomplishment, ambition is defined as greed.

Here's my clarification: greed is attempting to get something for nothing, to take without exchange.

Is getting the most money possible for the goods or services you deliver greed or intelligence? Is it greed or ambition? Are you a better person if you voluntarily get less money than you could for the goods or the services you deliver? No—in fact, you are derelict in your duty as business owner. You have a duty to yourself, your family, your investors or partners or shareholders, your lenders, your vendors, and your customers, and that responsibility is to attain the absolute highest and greatest profits possible, so you can stay in business successfully to honor every commitment to every one of these constituencies. To settle for anything less than the most is absolute dereliction of the responsibility of business ownership and leadership. To settle for anything less is to leave your business vulnerable, possibly fragile. And you should be fired.

Now, here's my question for you: what is your *entrepreneurial responsibility?* What is the entrepreneur's responsibility? What must you do in order to deserve and earn your place on the planet? Your success, prosperity, security, wealth?

A lot of people think your purpose, your responsibility in life is to provide jobs. You see that reflected in the communities that are busily trying to pass laws and, in some cases, communities and states suing companies to keep them from moving or closing; because their responsibility is to provide jobs to the community.

Is your responsibility to provide jobs? I hope you don't think so.

If providing jobs makes your business successful, if adding jobs makes it more successful, that's terrific. But if operating the business with fewer employees makes it more profitable, then it is your sworn responsibility as its captain to operate it with fewer employees.

A lot of people think your responsibility is to pay taxes.

Personally, I'd be a little happier with my gigantic income tax bill if the IRS sent me pictures, maybe of citizens of the foreign countries we support and of welfare recipients here in the United States; like when you send money to the starving orphan organization and you get the photograph and a letter once in a while about how they're doing. I think every taxpayer should get some of those and have people assigned to them. So for your money, you get a picture of 17 people in Iraq or Afghanistan or Gooblesedyburg where we're building roads and schools and providing food—which we do even for the populations of countries openly hostile to us, like North Korea—and of 4 welfare recipients and 1 retired guy, maybe from GM, so you can put photos of all the people you're supporting up on the refrigerator. And they should all have to write you notes every once in a while, to let you know how they're doing. I'd feel better. Wouldn't you?

You have a legal responsibility to pay the minimum taxes required of you.

But your responsibilities as entrepreneur do not include paying any more taxes than the minimum legally required of you. If you can arrange your business structure or affairs differently or relocate your business in order to pay fewer taxes, it is your sworn responsibility to do so.

Is it your responsibility to improve your customers' lives? No, it is not. Now, it's pretty smart to sell them things that, if they use them as you intended, will improve their lives. That's smart. But it's not your responsibility to see that it gets done. Nor should you lose any sleep over the customers who do not use what you sell them to improve their lives.

I had to come to grips with that in my businesses very early on, or I'd have had my wealth attraction severely suppressed. A lot of my wealth has been derived from writing and recording and publishing information products intended to help people better their attitudes, thinking, skills, businesses, and finances—just like this book. Frankly, the shrinkwrap never comes off a whole lot of what I sell. And you will kill yourself in my business if you worry about making them take off the shrinkwrap. The books never get read. The ideas never acted on. My clients very successfully sell perfectly good exercise equipment that gathers dust in buyers' garages, bottles of health-producing nutritional supplements that age unopened on closet shelves, business opportunities never worked on, heck, even vacation homes they rarely visit.

Should I feel guilty about the majority who pay their money but then never do anything with what they bought? Should I follow them home and refund their money? When I take a cruise, stay at a top-flight resort or buy another racehorse, I give no thought to whether the money paying for it came to me from someone who used what they bought or from someone who has never benefited at all. That's not my responsibility. It is theirs.

My preference is for you to actually read this entire book and extract from it ideas you act on and derive benefit from, but frankly that preference is based at least as much, if not more, on my profit motive, rather than your profit. Readers who do act on ideas turn out to be much better long-term customers.

Earlier in this book I mentioned having had a client who builds and installs deluxe, premium-priced backyard sheds. If his customer puts the shed in his backyard and never moves the crap out of the garage into the shed, and still can't park the car in the garage—or, more probably, he moves all of the crap out of the garage, into the shed, and then restocks the garage with more crap and still can't park the car in the garage—should my client go out there and give him his money back?

Of course not. In fact, he should go out there and sell him a second shed. Sell him garbage removal service. Sell him a how-to-do-a-garage-sale kit. *Sell him something.*

The entrepreneur's responsibility is this: maximum profit and wealth to his shareholders. If you're the sole shareholder, that's you. Then your responsibility is just to play fair, not lie, cheat, or steal. Integrity for the entrepreneur is optimizing sales and profits and value in the business he captains.

Just as the boxer who pulls punches in a championship fight lacks integrity, just as the quarterback who does not thoroughly prepare for the Super Bowl game lacks integrity, just as the lawyer who does not thoroughly prepare for trial and do everything he can for his client lacks integrity, just as the doctor who operates hung over lacks integrity, the business owner who "pulls his punches" also lacks integrity.

Are You "Guilty" of Opportunism?

Shortly after President George W. Bush sent our troops into Iraq, American Greetings Corporation rushed to the presses with a line of greeting cards to be sent to the military in Iraq. They created what they called the romantic ones, like one with a picture of a great-looking babe in a camouflage piece of lingerie, standing next to a bed. And the caption : "I've got some maneuvers to show you when you get home." There were war-themed cards for brothers, for sisters, for fathers, for mothers. The company got massive publicity as a result of this, including on *CNN, MSNBC, Entertainment Tonight, USA Today.*

They also drew criticism. I saw a critical discussion of this on some talk show. A liberal Hollywood celebrity attempting to launch a career as a political talking head railed about how horrible it was that this company was profiteering on the war. She contended, if, in fact, they are going to sell these things, they should be giving all the money away.

Of course, she, the show, and the network she was appearing on were also opportunists profiteering on exactly the same thing. The "story" of this outrage was their content, their programming, their product. She did not offer to donate her pay for the evening to a charity.

This is an illustration of a position often taken about this thing called opportunism. Truth is, everyone is opportunistic. Some are just better at it than others. The homeless beggar who discovers a dumpster filled nightly with exceptionally good leftovers and returns to it each night is an opportunist. If he keeps it secret and does not tell the other homeless folks about it, he's exceptionally opportunistic. I doubt this liberal denouncing the greeting card company would criticize the homeless person. Or recognize and acknowledge her own opportunism.

What is viewed as opportunism by many is entrepreneurship. That's what it is. Every man's tragedy is somebody else's opportunity. That's commerce.

I have clients in the fire alarm business. This business wouldn't exist if there weren't fires. You couldn't sell alarms if somebody wasn't having a house burn down around them. If there were no deaths, there'd be no business. In fact, the local sales organizations in this industry very opportunistically target neighborhoods immediately after a home has caught fire and burned to the ground.

They position their business as the mission to protect people, to save lives. That's how they sell what they sell. But their business wouldn't exist if it wasn't for the tragic problem in the first place.

But here's what's really important. If there weren't really appealing profits in the fire alarm business, the thousands of people whose lives are saved each year by having full-house fire alarm systems would, instead, be crispy critters. The fire alarm sales business is a difficult business. Appointments to visit with people in their homes, to discuss a subject no one is voluntarily interested in have to be obtained. Salespeople must be recruited, trained, and managed. This all requires considerable cost, investment, and patience. The salespeople must suffer a lot of rejection, must convince people to accept and act on a threat they prefer to ignore. A factory has to exist to manufacture alarms, requiring capital from investors.

None of that can happen without a lot of wealth to be had from this business.

So, the alarm that goes off at 2:00 A.M., that gets little Debbie, her Dad, Mom, and kitty-cat out of their house alive at 2:11 A.M., immediately before the entire home becomes a blazing inferno at 2:14 A.M. is on the wall of their home because a "greedy, opportunistic" fire alarm salesperson was in their home last week and delivered a high-pressure sales presentation with all the passion and persuasiveness he could muster.

So one man's tragedy is another man's opportunity. Entrepreneurship is all about opportunism.

A gas station raises its prices on the Friday before a holiday weekend. Is its proprietor an evil opportunist? What do you think? It's all part and parcel of what he must do in order to achieve maximum success in his business. At other times during the calendar year, there are price wars in his neighborhood and he sells his gas for less than it costs him in order to stay in business. If he's in an extremely competitive environment, he sells his gas at a loss the entire time in order to get business into his repair shop.

There are all sorts of fluctuations in his business. He'd better make maximum profits when the opportunity presents itself, in order to compensate for the times when he can't make any profit at all.

Consider the person who owns a convenience store in the middle of a gang-ridden ghetto, where nobody else will open a store. He mostly sells to people who can't get 20 miles away to the nearest supermarket. He sells at double what you would pay for the same products at the supermarket 20 miles away. Is he an evil opportunist? Well, would you go open a store there? If his store's not there, how do his customers get anything at all? His risk is much higher than the guy with the supermarket 20 miles away. Every time he works in the store, there's a very real chance somebody's going to walk in the door and blow his head off, or try. His theft rate is probably 400% or 500% worse than the supermarket's. For assuming all of that added risk, shouldn't he be an opportunist?

Getting all this stuff about greed and opportunism out of your head is critical. As an entrepreneur, you have a particular role in the world. You are a vitally important economic force. You have certain real responsibilities you need to embrace, illegitimate responsibilities others would impose you must reject. You also have rewards you deserve and should embrace.

Wealth Magnet 5
No Fear

I s *there a "dirty little secret" behind many wealthy* entrepreneurs' success stories?

Yes, but probably not any that would instantly pop in to most people's minds. Some people think it's luck or who they knew or rich relatives or disreputable behavior, somehow taking ruthless advantage of others, climbing to wealth by stepping on others. It is none of those things.

It is a past bankruptcy. Or at least a huge failure and wipe-out and near bankruptcy experience.

I've worked closely, personally, with hundreds of first generation, from-scratch millionaire and multi-millionaire entrepreneurs. Nearly half have gone bankrupt before ultimately achieving lasting success and wealth. A significant number of

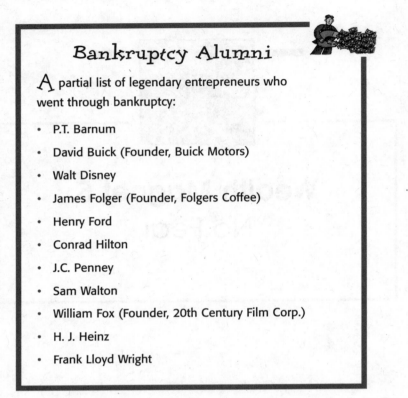

Bankruptcy Alumni

A partial list of legendary entrepreneurs who went through bankruptcy:

- P.T. Barnum
- David Buick (Founder, Buick Motors)
- Walt Disney
- James Folger (Founder, Folgers Coffee)
- Henry Ford
- Conrad Hilton
- J.C. Penney
- Sam Walton
- William Fox (Founder, 20th Century Film Corp.)
- H. J. Heinz
- Frank Lloyd Wright

legendary entrepreneurs have bankruptcies in their past. This is true of historical figures as well as contemporary ones. The incredible commonality among successful entrepreneurs is those who have been broke or formerly gone through bankruptcy.

There are reasons.

For one thing, **entrepreneurial success and wealth creation, as well as wealth attraction, requires a willingness to risk and experience failure, and the emotional resiliency to recover from it quickly, decisively, passionately, and persistently.** Hardly anybody gets to success via a straight line. So the past bankruptcy is revealing of this trait, or may have been instrumental in the development of this trait, or both.

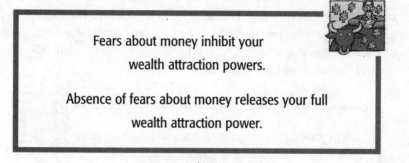

But more importantly, in my opinion, bankruptcy is one of those profound experiences that leads the entrepreneur to full and complete understanding of just how replaceable money is. When you experience a bankruptcy, as I have, you feel as if life is over, you'll never recover, you'll forever have a big red "B" on your forehead, you'll never get credit. Then when you discover none of that is true, and that money is readily available, wealth replaceable, more quickly and easily than the first time around, the light bulb comes on to full power. It's a huge "ah-ha!" and a giant "well, I'll be damned." From that moment onward, your fears about money are permanently banished and erased. What you feared was fatal turns out to be less than a flesh wound. Now you can't be scared again.

> Fears about money inhibit your
> wealth attraction powers.
>
> Absence of fears about money releases your full
> wealth attraction power.

Everyone who is anyone of achievement and wisdom counsels us against fear. Jesus Christ counseled against fear. Pope John Paul II counseled against fear. The pioneer in self-improvement, Earl Nightingale, pointed out that most of the things we worry endlessly about never occur except in our own negative imaginations. Napoleon Hill wrote, in the classic *Laws of Success,* about the ghosts of fear. The President wrote speeches for whom he goaded America out of the Depression, and famously said "we have nothing to fear but fear itself."

Every client I've ever had who has made a fear-based business decision has later regretted it. Every time we say no to fear, we win.

It's important to understand that fear is learned. We are born with fears of falling, loud unknown noises, and snakes. Otherwise God sends us here completely free of fear. We learn our fears from other humans. We are conditioned to be fearful by what we hear and observe as children by the influences of fearful adults we associate with. The irrational nature of most fears is well illustrated by the fact that more people fear public speaking than fear debilitating illness or death. More people fear airplane travel than automobile travel even though factually, statistically, air travel is infinitely safer.

It is my observation and conviction that more people are more controlled and inhibited by their fears about money than by any other kind of fear. People fear not having it, but they also fear being changed by having it. They fear making poor decisions about it. They fear running out of it before they die. Most of all they fear losing it. The best of us, and even the wealthiest of us, still have a whole lot of emotional baggage and B.S. connected to money in our closets!

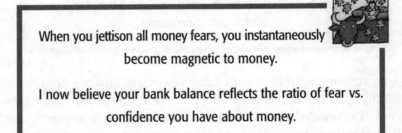

When you jettison all money fears, you instantaneously become magnetic to money.

I now believe your bank balance reflects the ratio of fear vs. confidence you have about money.

After my bankruptcy, which I feared would be fatal, I quickly discovered it was a mere bump in the road, and my fears were replaced by a rapidly growing confidence. Many years later, after considerable experience, my wife and I divorced, after 22 years of marriage. One half of all the wealth accumulated in the prior 10 years or so, a considerable amount, marched out the door with her. You could say it was at least 10 years of wealth. I easily replaced it in less than 18 months. I nearly doubled it in 24 months.

All of my prior experiences, including what I'd learned from my bankruptcy recovery, proved far more valuable than the actual money that moved out with her. I had zero fears about the loss of the money, about the difficulty of replacing it, about it having any adverse impact on my life or lifestyle. I just strolled over to the wall, adjusted the thermostat on my wealth attraction powers, and let the coffers refill, then overflow.

This is not to suggest license to behave recklessly or foolishly with your wealth. Waste, imprudence, irresponsibility is almost always punished, because such behavior is repulsive to money. But confidence magnetically attracts it, because confidence reflects real understanding and everyone and everything is attracted to understanding.

Consider an analogy: There's something you once did not understand, found incredibly difficult if not impossible to do, and hoped you would not encounter or have to deal with. Often there's some single, simple "trick" that changes everything. For example, if you attempt to assemble difficult jigsaw puzzles with a zillion pieces and you don't know that it helps enormously to build the outside four sides first, you may be stymied and frustrated until somebody takes pity on you and shows you that trick. The "oh, now I understand!" moment is wonderful, isn't it? Well, here's the trick about money. The understanding that it is available in unlimited supply and readily replaceable changes everything.

From Recession to New Economy

People who lived through The Great Depression kept a "Depression mentality" their entire lives. They stored and hoarded, they were debt averse, they squeezed the last drop from every tube, repaired rather than replaced anything that might be patched together and made to limp along just a little further. Such thrift is not necessarily a bad thing, and I think our modern society could benefit from a little more of it. The ease and speed with which we dispose of every imaginable thing troubles me. This kind of thrift taken to extremes, however, represents some inner, emotional scarring. It speaks of fear. In business, a certain level of prudent paranoia, of considering worst-case scenarios, and intelligent scheming to avoid them or ensuring against them is necessary, just as it is in ordinary life. If you choose to build a home at the ocean in an area of reoccurring risk of storms, even hurricanes, then you are foolish and irresponsible if you do not equip that home with storm shutters, perhaps a power generator, and do not buy appropriate insurance. But when this rises to the level of outright fear, it is unhealthy and harmful. If, for example, you went your whole life without ever even visiting the great beaches to see and experience the oceans, out of fear of the possibility of hurricane, you accept *rule of fear*. If you time your vacation to Florida or the Caribbean to avoid high hurricane season, you're prudent. **You should be prudent about money. You can't afford to be fearful about money.** The recent years' recession instilled new fears about money in a lot of people too young to have any experience with anything but a booming, expanding economy. Other, older people had let that experience fade to distant memory, but had all their old fears reignited.

Incidentally, as point of comparison, during the Depression over 9,000 banks failed, unemployment topped 25%, there were long "bread lines," and hundreds of thousands roamed the countryside, homeless itinerants in search of any work of any duration. During this most recent recession, the lines to buy the latest iPod or video game were long, not the bread lines. This time around, the destruction of the American economy has been greatly exaggerated. I'd further add that the tactic the media relies on to attract its wealth is mushrooming and magnifying every news event into Crisis. This is how they attract viewers, listeners, and readers, which is what they sell to advertisers—just as the carnival barker of old hollered about the horrific three-headed sea monster or giant King Kong-like creature inside the tent, to draw curious customers and take their quarters. Don't mistake most of what you see and hear in broadcast media these days as "news." It's nothing of the sort.

As we move into the post-recession New Economy, many new kinds of opportunities will present themselves, a great deal of temporarily idle and sidelined wealth will be liberated and begin moving about again with renewed vigor, and ultimately some sectors will again be affected by what Alan Greenspan dubbed "irrational exuberance" and "bubbles" will build and burst. Wealth will be attracted by many, retained and sustained by only some. So it has always been. So it always will be. You can never afford to fear this, nor should you let yourself be irrationally carried away by it.

To prosper in The New Economy, you must combine the never-changing principles and forces governing the movement of money with rational thought, reasoned optimism, creative vision, sound and timely strategy, and aggressive opportunism. Learn whatever lessons you can about prudent behavior from recent events. But do not learn fear.

Wealth Magnet 6
No Excuses

F ew people are attracted to whiners, complainers, excuse-makers, wimps. Hanging out with a victim is not appealing to most reasonably sane people. Who wants to be around or involved with an emotional cripple? The person in the victim shirt tends to wear out his welcome early. As he should. His thinking, his beliefs, and his behavior are even more repellant to money and wealth than they to other people.

In the *No B.S. Business Success* book, I explain that power is derived from taking responsibility, weakness from disavowing it. Here, again I want to emphasize as strongly as I can that wealth is attracted by taking responsibility, repelled by disavowing it.

It is interesting and a bit frustrating to me to watch the debate over the gap between worker and top executive compensation in

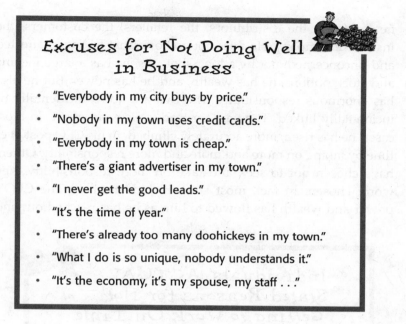

Excuses for Not Doing Well in Business

- "Everybody in my city buys by price."
- "Nobody in my town uses credit cards."
- "Everybody in my town is cheap."
- "There's a giant advertiser in my town."
- "I never get the good leads."
- "It's the time of year."
- "There's already too many doohickeys in my town."
- "What I do is so unique, nobody understands it."
- "It's the economy, it's my spouse, my staff . . ."

corporate America play out, especially the strident complaints about extraordinarily high CEO pay. What the argument ignores is the responsibility differential. The pay differential is admittedly extreme, but the responsibility differential is still more extreme. A manufacturing company is a good example. The company makes, ships, sells, and delivers dangerously defective doohickeys, which must now be recalled, costing the company and its shareholders millions of dollars, putting it at a competitive disadvantage in the marketplace, thus furthering the economic damage and harming the ability of its distributors, retailers, and salespeople to make their livings. The worker on the assembly line and the factory supervisors get off scot free, with zero responsibility. They do not need to give back any of their pay or perks, they go home that Friday unaffected and unconcerned, without penalty. The CEO winds up with all the responsibility. He must answer to his board, the shareholders, Wall Street, the news media, the distributors, the retailers, the customers, the insurance company. He does not go home that Friday unaffected and unconcerned, not by a long shot. Yes, he has a large income and stock options, he has wealth, and he has power. But he also has enormous responsibility. The two are not coincidentally or incidentally linked. They are, instead, cause and effect. In most cases, he has risen, more accurately climbed. to his CEO post over time by taking on more and more and more responsibility. Others have chosen not to seek and take on more responsibility. Key word: chosen. In fact, most shirk it, hide from it. The CEO's power and wealth has flowed to him as he has reached out and

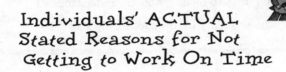

Individuals' ACTUAL Stated Reasons for Not Getting to Work On Time

Woody Allen said that half of success is showing up. The other half is showing up on time. These are people's excuses for being unable to show up on time.

- "Sometimes my car won't start."
- "The damned bus driver comes early."
- "I can't hear the alarm clock."
- "The dog hides my shoes."
- "I just can't get going. I'm not a morning person."
- "My mother was never a morning person." (It's mom's fault I can't get to work on time.)
- "It's unfair to ask somebody to be there at exactly the same time every morning."

grabbed more and more responsibility. He has also taken on greater and greater risk. It is his willingness to take on the responsibility that has brought him his wealth and power.

In the world of the entrepreneur, there is even clearer correlation between the taking on of responsibility and risk and the attraction of opportunity and wealth. If, as the saying goes, you aren't up for the heat, you'd best stay out of the kitchen. But if you opt to stay somewhere cool and comfortable, you ought not begrudge the goodies gobbled up by the big lads willing to stand in the fire.

Take a look at any year's *Forbes 400* list of the richest men and women, and ask yourself how many of those people have enjoyed "cool and comfortable." This truth needs to be told, often and vigorously, to the public, to counter the voices that demonize the rich and decry the giant incomes and wealth attracted and achieved by a minority in society. It needs to be thoroughly and deeply understood by anyone with serious ambition for wealth. You just can't go through life refusing to pay more than $3.00 for a meal and bitterly complain about only being able to dine out at McDonalds and resenting and vilifying those eating steak and drinking fine wine down the street at Morton's. They choose to pay Morton's prices. It's equally unreasonable for someone to go through life unwilling to meet the requirements for attracting wealth but being bitterly unhappy with the lack of it, and resentful and enraged at others who are willing to meet those requirements.

I, for example, have routinely earned over a million dollars a year as a freelance advertising copywriter, commanding per-project fees from $25,000.00 plus royalties for a single ad or sales letter up to $150,000.00 to even $1-million for complex, multi-step, multi-media project work. I'm often asked by other, much less wealthy copywriters what they need to do to get such fees. When I tell them what they must do to be worth such fees and make themselves attractive to the clients who can and will pay such fees, the blood visibly drains from their faces, they shake their heads, they walk away. For example, I tell them how extremely well-read legendary ad man David Ogilvy was, the hours he worked, the amount of self-promotion he engaged in. I tell them the advice I got from famous copywriter Gary Halbert—which I followed—about rewriting in longhand at least 500 long-running, successful direct-response ads and sales letters in order to train your subconscious mind. I tell them about the need to be a marketing strategist, not just a copywriter accepting assignments. I tell them about the attractant power of becoming a dynamic professional speaker and presenting speeches and seminars that showcase your expertise; becoming a persuasive author and getting articles and books published that also show-case your expertise and develop reputation. And on and on and on. I find few want to hear any of this. They just want to hear how to "get my kind of fees." They are unwilling to understand that it is impossible to "get" such fees, period. You must attract them, and that is a much more complicated thing.

I also often work under intense deadline pressure, work long hours, occasionally pull an all-nighter. My family makes great sacrifices as I disappear into my basement cave even on sunny Sunday mornings, not to be seen until dinner, while other families spend the day at the park or zoo or baseball game. I tell those asking how to get my kind of fees that there is a lifestyle sacrifice and discipline and unique responsibility required.

It's also worth noting that, just as with the high-paid CEO of the manufacturing company discussed above, in my copywriter-strategist role, I am in a very hot place. Under enormous pressure and stress and scrutiny, with great responsibility. Not only is my client paying me a hefty fee, he is then risking much larger sums on implementing what I provide. At times, the life or death of a new product's launch or the success or failure of his entire business may hang in the balance. With regard to my own career, my reputation for delivering exceptional results, reliably, is my only

"We just haven't been flapping them hard enough."

asset, and it can easily be destroyed by just one spectacular failure—much as a movie producer's or actor's bankability may be destroyed by one box office bomb, regardless of the previous string of blockbuster successes. Ultimately, I am held responsible not just for those things I have very direct control over, such as the ideas I choose to use and the words I choose to put on paper conveying those ideas, but I am also held responsible for things over which I have little or no control—from news events occurring the week the magazine my ad is run or the client's staff's handling of inbound phone calls from prospects responding to my ads. Is that fair? I guess not, but it is what it is. And it is one of the reasons why some people attract wealth and others do not—their willingness to take on responsibility even extending to things over which they do not have control.

Pressure–Prosperity Link

As an entrepreneur, you are going to screw up. And you are going to have bad things happen on your watch that you actually had no hand in, or feel you couldn't possibly prevent. That's a given. What's important to understand is that the world watches and responds to the way you handle these situations. If you blame others, blame circumstances, offer up excuses, you telegraph weakness. If you step up, accept responsibility, offer no excuses, roll up your sleeves and work, you telegraph strength and command respect. With excuse-making, you may obtain some sympathy and pity but at the price of respect. And wealth is never transferred based on pity. It moves based on respect. Wealth attraction power has a great deal to do with self-respect and respect of others, and that has a great deal to do with your acceptance, even your embrace of responsibility.

Bill Rancic spoke at one of our Glazer-Kennedy Insider's Circle™ Member conferences. Bill was the first season winner on Donald Trump's TV show *The Apprentice*. He was a very successful entrepreneur pre-Trump, and had many valuable insights and experiences to share from his other businesses as well as his year with The Donald. One such story was about one of his earliest businesses, as a kid, cleaning and readying boats in a resort area for the seasonal arrival of their owners. Things went horribly awry, and, as he said, most kids would have cut and run or blamed the circumstances involved. He did not. He took an arguably unjustified 100% of the responsibility for himself, with the direct result of impressing and keeping all his customers, but also the more important indirect result of strengthening his over-all wealth attraction power. It paid off in the short-term in customers retained and renewed the next season, and in referrals. It paid off even bigger in the long-term in strengthening Bill's over-all wealth attraction power.

Losers are wealthy with excuses, moth-eaten, empty wallets, heads full of excuses. This is not an enviable wealth. An abundance of excuses guarantees a paucity of money. If excuses roll willingly from a person's tongue, it's certain money does not flow easily into his pockets. I've often said I can estimate a person's bank balance if he'll tell me about the books he reads and the people he hangs out with. But it's even easier to accurately estimate his bank balance if I hear the excuses he makes. The habit of excuse making is the worst of all habits.

If you remember the wonderful Pink Panther movies with Peter Sellers, you'll remember his Asian houseboy, whom he paid to attack him without warning, to keep him on his toes. I've been told by good authority that the boxer Mike Tyson once hired a man to walk behind him saying, "You the man, Mike, you the man." (There's a clue how Tyson could zip through a hundred million dollars and be broke.) A fine investment would be hiring a big, strong guy to walk around with you for a month carrying a stout baseball bat and every time you voiced an excuse, hauling off and knocking you into next week. I imagine you'll be unwilling to make that investment, so, instead, you might try keeping a little notebook in your pocket, to keep a diary of every excuse you catch yourself making for the next month, as well as every excuse you get from anyone else. Awareness automatically improves performance, so just the act of keeping the diary, and stopping whatever you're doing each time you proffer an excuse will have positive impact. Getting whacked silly by the strong man with the Louisville Slugger would have more impact but admittedly the side effects are problematic.

If you recall the cartoon character Popeye, you'll remember that he pumped up his strength and power when needed by gulping down a can or two of spinach. I think of that as a visual analogy; for the entrepreneur, responsibility is spinach. If you want to turn on wealth attraction power, gulp down some more.

There are no victims. Only volunteers.

—Lee Milteer, author of *Success Is an Inside Job*,
www.leemilteer.com

"... in 1969, only one year out of graduate school, I had the good fortune to work for W. Clement Stone. At the time he was a self-made multimillionaire worth $600 million. He was also America's premier success guru. He was the publisher of *Success* magazine, author of *The Success System That Never Fails*, and co-author with Napoleon Hill of *Success Through a Positive Mental Attitude*.

When I was completing my first week's orientation, Mr. Stone asked me if I took 100% responsibility for my life. "I think so," I responded.

"This is a yes or no question, young man. You either do or you don't."

"Well, I guess I'm not sure."

"Have you ever blamed anyone for any circumstance in your life? Have you ever complained about anything?"

"Uh . . . yeah . . . I guess I have."

"Don't guess. Think."

"Yes, I have."

"OK then. That means you don't take 100% responsibility for your life. Taking 100% responsibility means you acknowledge that you create everything that happens to you. It means you understand that you are the cause of all your experience. If you want to be truly successful, and I know you do, then you will have to give up blaming and complaining and take total responsibility for your life—that means all your results, your successes, and your failures. This is a prerequisite for creating a life of success . . . you see, Jack, if you realize that you have created your current conditions, then you can uncreate them and recreate them at will. Do you understand that? Are you willing to take 100% responsibility for your life?"

"Yes, sir, I am!—and I did."

—JACK CANFIELD, CO-AUTHOR OF CHICKEN SOUP FOR THE SOUL. FROM HIS BOOK THE SUCCESS PRINCIPLES, WWW.JACKCANFIELD.COM, WWW.THESUCCESSPRINCI-PLES.COM

Wealth Magnet 7
Speak Money

Most people speak lack, poverty, inadequacy, doubt, and fear.

You have to be careful about the vocabulary you use because every word thought, spoken, or written, if inner-directed, constitutes programming, instructions to your subconscious mind. It is overly simplistic to believe that what you say in your head (think) and speak out loud manifests. The title of Napoleon Hill's most famous book *Think and Grow Rich* is slightly misleading; more accurately it should be *How To Think to Grow Rich*. Thought alone will not override behavior or certain physical realities and circumstances. However, it is accurate to say that the way you think about money and the language you use about money matters a great deal. How you speak about money reveals the programming your subconscious is actually being directed by; and your subconscious is accumulating programming to which it is trying to respond. Further, your spoken words convey to others your relative comfort and confidence or discomfort and fear about money. Any sales professional can tell you that prospects "smell fear" like animals. This is not superstition on their part. Experienced sales pros know it is infinitely harder to make the sale you desperately feel you must make than the sale that doesn't matter much one way or the other. Professional negotiators all know that the person who wants it least has the power. Money is naturally attracted to the person most confident and comfortable about it.

People tend to transfer their money to these same people. When you are talking to others, there's text and subtext, heard by others' conscious and subconscious minds. When you say that you just don't "feel good" about somebody or that your "intuition" tells you not to trust or do business with somebody, it's your subconscious processing impressions from sight, sound, the other senses, searching its files for past information and experiences. You can't actually enunciate why you feel as you do. You just do. So you might not consciously realize that when you're around Joe he often talks in terms of lack, poverty, failure, and fear, so you do not want to buy from him, invest with him, or otherwise be involved with him. But that may very well be what has occurred within your subconscious.

For all these reasons, what you speak about money matters.

As an example, consider the term: "Hard-earned dollars." You all recognize the term, don't you? Hard-earned dollars. You probably heard your parents say it. Your friends may say it. You may say it, or some variation of it, without ever considering its true meaning. If you translate it to programming, it is: money is very hard to get. You get money only through difficult and unpleasant work. If money somehow arrives without being connected to hard work, there's something wrong with it. It's tainted or toxic. It's incorrect and dishonorable to get it easily.

Now consider the phrase "easy money." For most people, this is "bad." The perception is that "easy money" is somehow tainted, dirty, undeserved. The perception is that the person seeking "easy money" is a lazy bum or a fool.

What a barrier! This is a tall, wide, thick wall that prevents entrepreneurs from looking for or seeing many great opportunities in their own businesses, lying there within easy reach. I think this explains why a pair of fresh, expert eyes like mine can so easily and frequently see unexploited opportunities in others' businesses. It's not just that the owner of the business is too close to the trees to see the forest. There's a wall he can't see through at all.

What a barrier! If things start to get easy, if money starts flowing in faster, in bigger sums than ever before, the entrepreneur will subconsciously reject it and engage in all manner of self-sabotage to slow the unjust flow.

The fact is, there's no reason money has to be hard to earn or earned in hard ways. I've taught thousands of entrepreneurs how to earn much larger incomes more easily. There are so many ways this can occur, a hundred books couldn't chronicle them all. I'll try, though, to give you a sense of the range.

For example, there's Dr. Chris Tomshack, who had developed an extraordinarily effective marketing system for attracting patients to his chiropractic practice; on the back of this system, he went from owning and operating one clinic to two to three to four. But there he hit the wall. He found himself spread too thin trying to manage four clinics as well as one. He became frustrated by declining quality, burdened by more and more time going to managing staff and being taken away from his expert attention to advertising and marketing, and ended up actually working harder and harder for less and less. Expansion from four to six to ten was unimaginable. At my suggestion, he switched to franchising and, as of this writing, his company, HealthSource, has over 240 franchised chiropractic and weight-loss clinics throughout America, his income leapt from a very hard-earned six figures to a much more easily and pleasantly earned seven figures, and he is positively affecting the health of hundreds of thousands instead of thousands. Make no mistake, his life is not absent of work. He is now CEO of a fast-growing company, recognized by national magazines for its meteoric growth. But his work is not the "hard work" most think of, and his financial rewards have no proportionate connection whatsoever to hours worked or numbers of patients treated with his hands. His wealth is not limited by his own work, or by his ability and tolerance for hands-on management, or even by geographic boundaries.

My client Dennis Tubbergen has changed the way thousands of upper-tier financial advisors secure clients and earn millions in fees and commissions, with the switch from arduous one-on-one prospecting and presentations to small-group "focus groups" for qualified prospective clients, effectively leveraging the same work to a power of 8 to 12.

Diana and Pierre Cotu, in a field dominated by low prices—pizza—focused on upscale, gourmet products, with their average large pizza priced from $22.00 to $38.00. The work of delivering 100 pizzas is virtually the same at their pizzeria as it is at, say, Pizza Hut or Dominos, but the profit is substantially greater. Their business doubled, by the way, in a peak year of the recent recession.

Another client, Owen Garrett, a pencil artist, decided not to sell his art in traditional ways, like exhibiting weekend after weekend after weekend from morning to night at community art shows or endlessly soliciting and "working" gallery owners for a few spaces on their walls or a show now and then. Instead, Owen focused on the corporate market, where companies buy his works in series, collections, and in quantity, on a continuous basis, as client gifts and awards. He also used the internet, a newsletter, and other direct marketing media to build his own passionate, loyal following of fans who eagerly await his next new life-adventure and the artworks it inspires. As I write this,

deck or in my big leather recliner in my library. Counting travel days and speaking days, in 1996, it required more than 200 days to earn what only 42 days provided in 2004. Considerably easier, less strenuous, less stressful days. This shift involved procedural changes in my business, changes in strategy, but also, of equal importance, continuous improvement of my thinking, under-standing, even imaginings about money.

Breaking free of the Work-Money Link has not been easy for me. I was raised to have enormous respect for work ethic. My youth experiences taught me that money is hard earned and earned hard. Shaking that, replacing that thinking is no simple trick. But that link is an illusion, not a reality.

This is not to suggest that I don't work or that you shouldn't. In fact, I think work of some kind is necessary for sound mental and physical health. But there is work and then there is *work*. My Platinum Member Ron LeGrand's motto is "The Less I Do, The More I Make." It is subject to misinterpretation. It is meant as a variation on the "work smarter, not harder" theme. Personally, I work at working on my terms, on things that I enjoy, on high-yield opportunities and tasks, and I coach others to do the same. I am all about finding ways to make things easier, not harder. To do more with less. To gain leverage. But if you think and speak the belief of "hard-earned dollars," you reinforce a barrier to doing any of these things.

This is just one example of hundreds of negative, limiting statements routinely thought and said about money. They are all bricks strengthening and reinforcing the wall between you and attraction of maximum wealth.

What You Speak Reveals What You Are

Do you have kids? And how many times, in the past month, did you explain to the kids that money doesn't grow on trees? Where's that come from? Maybe you've become your father.

Maybe you are simply repeating what you've always heard. It's been programmed in. And now, at a particular point in your life, you are regurgitating it and spitting it back out with no thought about what it's doing to you or what it's doing to the person that you're saying it to. When you say this, what belief system is it communicating and reinforcing?

I am not for spoiling kids; that's another discussion for another time and place. For now, let's keep the harsh spotlight focused on you. When something like that spews out of your mouth, it came from somewhere. It came from your own mind, your subconscious, your belief system, the recordings that play inside your head. Whatever you say about money is simultaneously revealing and reinforcing.

There is a unique language used by wealth-attracting entrepreneurs. I hear it all the time, because I hang out and work with them most of the time. I've been surrounded by them for years. They speak one language, the outside world speaks another. I'm not going to hand you a vocabulary list here and suggest you try memorizing it, or suggest you read positive affirmations 20 times a day from 3-by-5-inch cards. That can be useful, but it is a tiny piece of this puzzle, and overly simplistic. Trying to use a vocabulary list won't cut it. The language has to be an honest, natural reflection of your beliefs about money and wealth; everything in this book has to come together and support the changes you choose to make in your own belief system.

But make no mistake: What you speak matters. And you can attract more wealth more easily by speaking the language of wealth.

Trump-Speak

Not since Muhammad Ali went around yelling "I AM THE GREAT-EST" has anybody become so famous for hyperbolic, superlative statements about himself and everything he does, as has The Donald. With almost every breath, he declares something made-by-Trump as the biggest, the grandest, the greatest, the most amazing, the most successful. Listen to him speak about his TV shows *The Apprentice* and *Celebrity Apprentice* and you'd think there were no others. When we had Trump's daughter, Ivanka, come and speak at one of the Glazer-Kennedy Insider's Circle™ Super-Conferences (the name, a bit of hyperbole of our own) and I sat in the backstage "green room" with her, I immediately noticed the exact same Trump-Speak as she described the real estate projects she was working on and her jewelry line. So I asked her about it. She said she'd grown up with it, it was ingrained and natural, and was a way not just of promotion, but of re-affirming commitment to an ideal and a position in the world. "After all, if we can't make what we're doing the best," she said, "why would we choose to do it?" I believe "Trump-Speak" reflects a deeply felt ideal, the more often and consistently spoken, the more deeply felt. A closed loop of extreme confidence construction for self and assertive, pre-eminent positioning to the marketplace.

Donald Trump has been asked about this himself many times. In his own words . . .

> ". . . key to the way I promote is BRAVADO. People may not always think big themselves but they get very excited by those who do. People want to believe something is THE biggest and THE greatest and THE most spectacular.

"Some people have written that I'm boastful, but they are missing the point. If you're devoting your life to creating a body of work and you believe in what you do, and what you do is excellent, you'd damn well better tell people you think so. Subtlety and modesty are appropriate for nuns, but if you're in business, you'd better learn to speak up and announce your significant accomplishments to the world."

Wealth Magnet 8
Be Somebody

*B*e a famous somebody. Like it or not, we live in a celebrity-obsessed culture, a celebrity-driven marketplace.

In recent years, my clients in the seminar and conference business have dramatically increased attendance or total onsite revenues or both by adding celebrity speakers to their events, including Donald Trump and Dr. Phil. At our own Glazer-Kennedy Insider's Circle™ conferences, we usually feature a celebrity-CEO or celebrity-entrepreneur, such as Gene Simmons (KISS), George Foreman, Jim McCann (1-800-Flowers), Ivanka Trump, and Joan Rivers. And for 9 years I spoke on the biggest seminar tour ever, in 25 to 29 cities a year, to audiences of 10,000 to 35,000, in arenas, with speakers like former Presidents Ford, Reagan and Bush, Generals Colin Powell and Norman

Schwartzkopf, Larry King, Bill Cosby, and dozens more from Hollywood, sports, politics, and business. Stadiums were filled for business seminars as if they were rock concerts because of the drawing power of these celebrities. My client of many years, the Guthy-Renker Corporation, changed the infomercial industry forever when it began using celebrity hosts and testimonials in its TV infomercials. Even *Forbes* magazine now publishes an annual issue all about the wealthiest and most influential celebrities, and it sells just as well as its annual issue about the richest business leaders. No matter your market—CEOs or ditch-diggers, young or old, poor or super-affluent—it is influenced by and attracted to celebrity.

So it is smart to make yourself into a celebrity.

Not necessarily the kind who appears on *Oprah* or the cover of *People,* but a celebrity within your own business sphere, your own market, whether that's defined geographically, demographically, by particular industry or profession, or otherwise. The smaller the universe, the easier it is to be a celebrity. Arnold Schwarzenegger was first a celebrity in the niche world of bodybuilding, from which he extracted a great deal of wealth, before the general public was even aware of his existence. Many of my clients are famous celebrities in their own industries, quite likely to be stopped and asked for their autographs, or collect a crowd at their industry conventions, yet you would neither recognize their faces nor know their names.

At a local level, it is relatively easy for a businessperson to achieve celebrity status, in large part merely by making himself a focal point of all his advertising. Quite a few of our Members have successfully created local celebrity status or niche celebrity status for themselves. In Edmonton, Canada, Dr. Barry Lycka is a bona fide celebrity. When he offers an open seminar or special event, hundreds attend. He has long featured himself in extensive newspaper, TV, and direct-mail advertising for both his practice and his spa. My client, Darin Garman, a commercial real estate broker and developer, has attracted investors to Iowa real estate from all over the world by making it all about him, and making himself into a celebrity with his "Former Iowa Prison Guard Discovers . . ." story. Diana of Diana's Gourmet Pizzeria has made a point of competing in—and sometimes winning—national and international chef competitions, generating considerable publicity in her local media and even on The Food Network. In every case, these businesspeople elevate their status by writing books, publishing newsletters, putting on events, and learning to use the media effectively to generate publicity for themselves and their businesses, and feature themselves in their advertising.

Local celebrity can lead to national celebrity. A one-time client of mine, Dr. Robert Kotler, a Beverly Hills cosmetic surgeon, began making himself a '"celebrity doctor" with the local advertising of his self-published book *The Consumers' Guide to Cosmetic Surgery* and Los Angeles media appearances made possible by the book. Recently, he was a featured doctor in the reality TV series aired nationally on the E network, *Dr. 90210*.

Certainly within your own clientele, it is easy to become a celebrity—and doing so will improve customer or client retention, spending, and referrals. To your own clientele, you build your own celebrity status through self-aggrandizement, self-promotion, and association with celebrities. *Any* association. Any and every photo of you with a celebrity has real value to you. Many of our Members get photo opportunities at our events with the likes of Gene Simmons and Ivanka Trump, and these photos quickly migrate to their websites, newsletters, and with news releases, to their local or niche media, along with their reports of meeting these people used in their blogs, Facebook, Twitter, and so on.

There are several reasons for making yourself a celebrity in the eyes of your customers, prospects, and local media. It makes you more interesting to them. They are curious about you and about your encounters with celebrities. It gives your clientele bragging rights and cocktail party conversation fodder—they enjoy talking about *their* doctor, financial advisor, restaurant owner, dog groomer, whoever is the one people have seen on TV, heard on radio, read about in the newspaper or who just came back from the international pizza-making competition in Rome, Italy, or a major business conference where they hung out with Gene Simmons of KISS . . . imagine that! You not only make yourself more attractive from a marketing standpoint by making yourself a celebrity, you actually add value for your clients or customers.

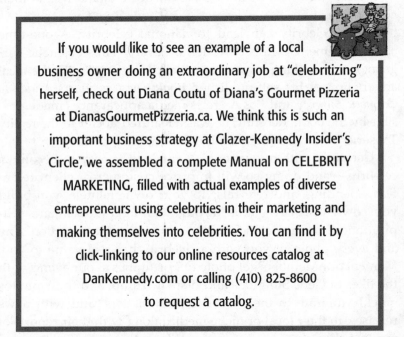

If you would like to see an example of a local business owner doing an extraordinary job at "celebritizing" herself, check out Diana Coutu of Diana's Gourmet Pizzeria at DianasGourmetPizzeria.ca. We think this is such an important business strategy at Glazer-Kennedy Insider's Circle,™ we assembled a complete Manual on CELEBRITY MARKETING, filled with actual examples of diverse entrepreneurs using celebrities in their marketing and making themselves into celebrities. You can find it by click-linking to our online resources catalog at DanKennedy.com or calling (410) 825-8600 to request a catalog.

Be an Expert Somebody

Expert status is very magnetic. Fortunately, it is a self-created, self-manufactured asset.

The great success educator Earl Nightingale said you could make yourself a world-class expert in most fields simply by studying every available resource for an hour a day for just a year. I took him seriously. I made myself into a top expert in the field of direct marketing entirely through self study, with no academic or experience qualifications whatsoever, in less than three years, and charged high fees from the very beginning. I have also successfully positioned myself as a marketing expert in several specialized fields—for example, well over 10,000 chiropractors and dentists have attended my practice-building seminars, bought my books and courses on practice marketing, been in coaching programs, etc. I built the largest seminar and publishing company serving these professions in the early '80s, I've been hired to speak for five different, major practice-building companies as well as state dental and chiropractic associations, and was once named "Practice Guru of the Year" by a major trade journal in dentistry, yet I'm neither a chiropractor nor a dentist.

I am fond of a quote I got from a fellow direct-response copywriter John Francis Tighe: "In the land of the blind, the one-eyed man is king." If you know more about "x" than your intended clientele, you ARE an expert! It is very important to understand that giving yourself expert status and presenting yourself as an expert has little, if anything, to do with securing permission from authority figures or collecting alphabet soup designations, certifications, and diplomas from others. In most cases, the marketplace does not discriminate between such "official" recognitions of expertise and self-manufactured declarations, representations, and demonstrations. This is very disconcerting and difficult to swallow for those who've devoted years to obtaining the official approval of others, but their refusal to differentiate between the way their peers judge expertise and the way the public understands expert status only gets in their way of attracting wealth. Peer approval very rarely makes anybody rich.

Obviously, everybody prefers working with experts. This is especially true as you climb the affluence ladder; the more affluent the customer, the more determined he is to find and conduct business with the most knowledgeable, respected, and celebrated expert, and the more willing he is to travel further away from home, wait longer, do business on your terms, and pay premium fees or prices. But really, everybody prefers dealing with an expert if and when they can. If you suffer from blinding headaches, and you can get to the doctor who wrote *The Official Guide To Drug-Free Headache Relief*, who has a newspaper column about headaches, which you've seen, who's on the radio, you would rather go see him about your problem than any other "ordinary" doctor.

In The New Economy, presenting yourself as an expert, and being accepted as an expert, is of multiplied importance. The recession experience has conditioned consumers to be more thoughtful, selective, and discriminating about how they spend their money and who they spend it with. So many lying to them and so many exposed as emperors with no clothes—including major Wall Street firms, giant banks and insurance companies, the venerable General Motors, as well as government agencies and, of course, politicians—has heightened skepticism. The New Economy customer is skittish about trusting anybody, trying to be more prudent about spending, and in greater need of reassurance. Expert status is reassurance.

Experts encounter less fee or price resistance, so, usually, they can charge premium prices, enjoy above-average profit margins, and, if they choose, derive greater income from fewer clients or customers. Because my client Darin Garman is an expert in profitable, "peace-of-mind" investing exclusively in heartland-of-America apartment buildings, he can attract investors from all over the world as well as dominate his local market in Iowa, charge an access fee and monthly membership fee just to be permitted to purchase properties from him, and never, never, never discount commissions. Because Bill Hammond's elder law practice specializes in working with families with a senior with Alzheimer's, his fees are at the top of the pyramid, mandatorily packaged and not available for cafeteria purchase, and rarely questioned. Of course, you may think you are not in a profession that lends itself to expert status. My contention is that every business does. So I could tell you very similar stories about carpet cleaners, lawn and garden companies, auto repair shops, even an industrial tarp manufacturer positioned as experts and specialists, prospering from carefully chosen target markets, selling their goods and services for 5 to 25 times their industry norms.

If you have a long memory, you may remember the Mr. Ed television show featuring the talking horse. A line in its theme song was: "A horse is a horse, of course, of course." But to horse owners, a horse is not a horse. I own about 20 harness racing horses, which are their own breed called Standardbred. These are the kind that race pulling two-wheeled racing carts called sulkies, and have drivers, not jockeys. The horses that race in the Kentucky Derby are a different breed, Thoroughbred. While both often retire to second careers as pleasure horses, trail riding horses, and even competitive jumping horses, there are other breeds more typically preferred by owners for those purposes. Owners of each kind of horse are suspicious of therapies or professionals used by owners of other types of horses, so those of us involved in harness racing much prefer veterinarians, equine chiropractors, and farriers who we know to be expert in caring for harness racing horses, as well as nutritional and therapy products made for harness racing horses and endorsed by top trainers of harness racing horses. Endorsements from top Thoroughbred trainers carry little weight with us, endorsements from top trainers in our world carry little weight with those in Thoroughbred racing— and if I were selling an ointment, liniment, or nutritional supplement perfectly suitable for both, I'd bottle it with two different names and labels and bring it to the separate markets from two different companies.

An important point to remember about self-manufactured expert status is that the smaller, narrower, and more specific the market you want to appeal to, the easier it is to fashion and present yourself as an expert in it, and to become known and accepted as such.

Wealth Magnet 9
Be Somewhere

I n the midst of one of his dark periods, when the news was filled with stories of his financial demise, Donald Trump talks about feeling like just staying hidden at home but instead strapping on his tuxedo and going to an important gala—because he knew he could not possibly gain by staying home. At a time, some 30 years or so ago, when I was captain of a company everyone in its industry knew to be in deep and dire financial circumstances, I considered skipping that year's convention. But I didn't. It might have been less stressful, less embarrassing, more comfortable to stay home. But I couldn't possibly gain by doing that. I went. I put myself in a place where it was at least possible that good, productive, profitable things could happen—and they did.

> ## Wealth won't find you if you are at home slouched on—or hiding under—the couch.

Hopefully, you aren't in the upside-down financial condition I was, or Donald Trump was, at the above-mentioned times. But regardless of your circumstances, you have to make a point of putting yourself in places where opportunity can occur. My father passed on a pair of cufflinks to me with the letters: **YCDB-SOYA.** They stand for: <u>Y</u>ou <u>C</u>an't <u>D</u>o <u>B</u>usiness <u>S</u>itting <u>O</u>n <u>Y</u>our <u>A</u>ss.

While this refers to personal movement and placement, such as the meetings and conferences and cocktail parties and community events you attend and make yourself visible at, it also goes far beyond that. As an example, consider this book, and the other 14 books I have written and had published. For more than 18 years, I have been on bookstore shelves without interruption. I have worked hard to make that happen. Why? I can assure you, not for the royalty income paid to me as an author; that represents less than 1% of my income. I want to be on those bookshelves because people discover me there—who might never discover me otherwise—and become Glazer-Kennedy Insider's Circle™ Members and newsletter subscribers, attend seminars, become private clients, or bring me other opportunities. Being there, on bookstore shelves, has both directly and indirectly enriched me by millions of dollars. I can specifically identify more than a dozen long-term clients who have each spent between $100,000.00 and $300,000.00 with me. I have been sought out for speaking engagements purely because a corporate executive bought and read one of my books. For me, Being Somewhere includes being on bookstore shelves, including this book, which is now in your office or home.

That does not mean you must write a book. It is an example of the wealth attraction power of being somewhere. Because the most important words in the above paragraph are "discover me" and "sought out." This is marketing by attraction.

Being Somewhere for the local insurance agent or financial planner, for example, might mean speaking to local groups of dentists, chiropractors, M.D.'s, and other high-income professionals; creating and mailing a good, informative, expert-position enhancing newsletter on financial matters to a targeted list of such prospects every month; appearing regularly on a local radio show; serving on the board of an important charity. Almost any entrepreneur can be somewhere via speaking, writing, publishing, networking, even serving, with it all carefully chosen to facilitate the right people taking notice and ultimately seeking him out for advice and information or bringing him new opportunities.

This gets us to the subject of "place."

Enormous wealth—and fame—often comes from re-location, not necessarily in the geographic sense, but in terms of media or market space. Comedienne Joan Rivers, with whom I did some writing and consulting work some years back, created an immensely prosperous business and a career renaissance and new fame by moving from stand-up comedy and regular TV to QVC, the home shopping network. That prominence and reputation as entrepreneur even led to her gig in the 2008 *Celebrity Apprentice*—which she won.

Several years ago, Harley-Davidson began focusing aggressively on women riders and buyers, and moved that sales activity out of their regular dealerships and showrooms to "garage parties" ala Tupperware.

During the recent recession, a number of my clients who had replaced trade show exhibiting, speaking at conferences, and organizing and conducting their own road-shows with introductory seminars or group demonstrations held in hotel meeting rooms in a string of cities with less cumbersome, less laborious media, like webinars, teleseminars, and video-conferencing were forced to go back out into the marketplace themselves or put sales representatives and sales teams back out on the road. Some found this retro relocation so profitable they are committed to continuing it post-recession, for the foreseeable future. Conversely, a client of mine, an attorney who specializes in ultra-sophisticated asset protection for affluent entrepreneurs and CEOs, who principally attracted clients by speaking at very select conferences, has recently found—as a pleasant surprise—that putting highlights of his lectures and some interviews on YouTube is bringing appropriate clients just as convinced of his elite expert status as those who encounter him as a lecturer at venues like cruises for wealthy investors, with workshops presented by financial, investment, and political authors.

In place strategy, there are obvious and non-obvious choices, and often the big breakthroughs come from the non-obvious.

One of the things I try to get every entrepreneur, marketer, and professional to think about is being in more places than anyone in their category of expertise or services typically puts himself. Most people are very limited, get comfortable with only a few places, and stay there. My advanced version of the "Be Somewhere Wealth Magnet" is: Be *everywhere* that's relevant, everywhere your ideal customer or clients are, and be omnipresent in those environments.

A list of my other books appears on page 243.

You can also preview sample chapters and excerpts of many of these books at www.NoBSBooks.com.

Your Wealth Attraction GPS

- **Out and about, not in and forgot!**

- **"Motion beats meditation." —Gary Halbert**

- **Where are your best prospective customers/clients/patients?** (What do they read? Watch? Listen to? Where do they go, congregate?)

- Where can you place yourself that **elevates your status and importance?**

- Where can you place yourself that **showcases and demonstrates your expertise?**

- **Who or what can you associate yourself with** that your best prospective customers/clients/patients pay attention to, respect, or are involved with?

- **Re-location can equal re-invention.** Strategies of "different place" provide new opportunities.

- **In place strategy, don't just settle for the obvious choices.** "Just 'cuz you're following a well-marked trail don't mean whoever made it knew where they were going." —Texas Bix Bender, author, *Don't Squat With Yer Spurs On*. Nor does it mean they cut the only trail or the best trail. And there may be a lot less traffic in your way on a different trail.

- **Omnipresence:** Once you decide on your "where," the best questions are: How many different ways can I appear there simultaneously? and How can I be there all the time?

Wealth Magnet 10
Do Something

My friend and business legend, *the late Gary* Halbert's favorite saying was: "Motion beats meditation." It would probably amaze a lot of people if they could know the inside story of a lot of "rags to riches" entrepreneurs' lives as I do, to discover that just about the only reason for their meteoric success was simply getting into motion, ready or not.

Recently, recession has brought on a whole new level of mental and emotional paralysis; businesspeople at all levels have been affected. This paralysis is juxtaposed with the growing importance of speed-to-market and agile, continuous change. In The New Economy, rewards will be taken by those who act. Those who have historically lagged behind and survived off crumbs left behind by leaders will now discover there aren't any crumbs left. More than ever, it's necessary to put premium and priority on *action*.

Some years ago, I had an opportunity to spend a day with Lee Iacocca, in my consulting work. I was thrilled to do so, as I had long studied him, his business methods, and his personal behavior. I often tell the entrepreneurs I coach about how highly Iacocca prizes decisiveness and action, a fact perhaps best illustrated by his story of the rebirth of the convertible at the financially troubled Chrysler. Iacocca led Chrylser back from the brink, restoring its profitability, marketplace strength, and even repaying loans guaranteed by the government ahead of schedule. Factory workers caught him walking around and suggested that one of the cars would make a great convertible. He told them to get a blowtorch, cut the roof off, let him drive it around and see how people reacted. And the rest, as they say, is history. The relaunch of the convertible by Chrysler probably attracted more media and public attention and brought more money to Chrysler at a faster pace than any other idea ever acted on in the company's history. All because there was that rare CEO in place who heard a good idea and immediately acted on it. No design committees, no focus groups, no endless meetings of engineers, no long-delayed prototype. *A blowtorch.*

Sadly, of course, all these years later, Chrysler found its way back to the brink of bankruptcy, as did the even more venerable giant, GM. There were many contributing factors, but two of the biggest were delaying and delaying and delaying actions on festering, cancerous problems; denial, denial and more denial about a changed and changing marketplace. In some respects, it's fitting that these companies became wards of the state, as they functioned for too long like government bureaucracies rather than like businesses. Ford fared better by doing more, more quickly. Its fate is still in question as I write this, but Ford is certainly the most likely to succeed of the three.

The lesson is that problems rarely improve with age. Opportunities wait for no one.

For the teleseminars and audio programs produced for Glazer-Kennedy Insider's Circle™ Members, I get to interview an eclectic mix of authors, experts, entrepreneurs, marketers, and innovators. One of my favorites has been an author I've long studied and admired, Robert Ringer. You may know him from his most famous best-selling book, *Winning Through Intimidation*, republished as *To Be or Not To Be Intimidated*. I rank it as one of the ten most influential books I have ever read, and credit it with directing me to my practice of "Takeaway Selling" described in a companion to this book: *No B.S. Sales Success for The New Economy*. When I interviewed Mr. Ringer about his newer book, titled *Action!: Nothing Happens Until Something Moves*, I said on the teleseminar, if you never read the book, but merely propped it up where you saw its cover everyday, you'd profit. Its title tells you exactly how so many of us attract abundant opportunity and wealth. *Movement.*

Free—you can hear a replay of the tele-seminar featuring my interview with Robert Ringer, author of *Action!*, online at www.NoBSBooks.com. Take action! Go there and listen.

I often say, if poor people knew how shockingly ordinary millionaires were, there'd be a lot more millionaires. One of the biggest erroneous ideas preventing poor people from getting rich is that the rich are somehow smarter or possess some "magic gene" that separates them from the masses in terms of aptitude or capability. Nothing could be further from the truth. I work very closely, day in and day out, with many millionaire and multi-millionaire entrepreneurs, and I assure you, we aren't that much smarter than the clerk at the corner convenience store. I have clients personally earning millions of dollars a year who forget to put on their shoes when they leave the house, have walked through the screen door on the front of my house without noticing it was there, are woefully dysfunctional managers, incredibly disorganized, slow readers, can't do math, etc. In fact, one, who has built a national chain of tax preparation offices serving hundreds of thousands of clients can't, himself, add two numbers together without a calculator and couldn't decipher a financial statement if you put a gun against his head. The richest real estate investor I work with was a car mechanic, another a prison guard. But there is one thing they all do that the vast majority of the population doesn't. The "little" difference is the subject of Ringer's book: these people take action.

In *Action!*, Robert Ringer wrote "I have always believed that the difference between success and failure, in any area of life, is not nearly as great as most people might suspect." I not only agree, I have abundant proof from the more than 100 "from-scratch" millionaires I've worked with, from their stumbling beginnings to their present wealth, celebrity, expert credibility, and achievements.

> The act of taking action is, in and of itself, a magnet for opportunity and wealth.

You've undoubtedly seen, in many movies, the guns with body-heat-seeking technology that make the person trying to hide appear in neon red or green, as he moves in the dark jungle, generating body heat. You've heard of heat-seeking missiles. There's a similar effect with action and wealth. **Wealth seeks movement.**

Over the years, I've found that just about everybody has at least one really good idea, skill, or talent that could translate to prosperity and success. I once briefly dated a divorced mother with three young kids, working in a low-wage factory job, barely staying one day ahead of bills. I discovered she occasionally

"Sheer will, I tell you—sheer will."

found time to paint—and my jaw dropped when I saw the paintings. I own racehorses, and there are several artists who have become famous in the racing industry as horse portrait artists. People routinely pay them thousands of dollars to paint portraits of their horses. Several sell their original paintings for tens of thousands of dollars. This woman's work was as good or better than any of those established and successful artists. As a marketing pro, without breaking a sweat, I was able to lay out a plan for her to enter this world, first locally, then nationally, and easily, quickly, make more money in a month than she was currently making all year—and achieve her stated number-one goal in life: to be a stay-at-home mom, there for her kids. Giving such free advice is almost always futile, as it was here. In fact, she had already thought of many of the things I suggested. But had never acted on those thoughts. And never will.

There are all sorts of reasons for this inaction. Poor self-image, lack of confidence, not being able to see yourself doing it. Ignorance. Laziness. Procrastination. Waiting for better timing, more resources. The list of excuses for inaction and status quo acceptance is long, and, of course, useless and valueless. If you seek to attract wealth into your life, you have to get the list out of your life.

I have had this exact same experience thousands of times. When I was doing interviews, appearances, and seminars for one of my previous books, *How To Make Millions with Your Ideas*, I had almost identical conversations with one person after another. Whenever someone finds out what I do, they tell me of their great idea that they've never acted on. Every cab and limo driver has a book he hasn't written and never will—although one did, and it led to the HBO series *Taxicab Confessions*. I once spoke at a very special, high-priced seminar for entrepreneurs, where experts in direct marketing via home shopping channels like QVC and HSN, infomercials, and radio all spoke and worked with about 100 attendees. Everyone there had an "idea" for a product that would be terrific for sale on QVC. None acted on their ideas except one, who subsequently sold millions of dollars worth of his invented item on QVC. Being the one that takes action is entirely a matter of choice.

Everybody has ideas. Everybody has latent talents. Everybody has ability.

Few act on them.

And make no mistake: There is no wealth to be found *in* an idea. There is only wealth to be had from acting *on* an idea.

This is so important, I want to relate several stories of people I work with, to illustrate the way they behave when presented with a worthy idea. The details of their businesses are not all that important, and you should avoid being distracted by them. Instead, focus on the way they responded to ideas and opportunities.

I mentioned Dr. Chris Tomshack earlier. He was an owner of four successful chiropractic practices when he was at a meeting of one of my coaching groups, with about 15 other clients, and we were discussing what each person thought of as the best aspects, assets, or strengths of their respective businesses, as well as their greatest frustrations and dislikes with their businesses. For each, I had a few pointed suggestions including a "big idea." In his case, it was escaping the day to day detail of practice and leveraging his outstanding marketing by franchising his clinic, something tried a few times but never successfully done in chiropractic. He went home, devised a plan, called, consulted with me, went home and went to work—and in the first 2 years zoomed to 240 franchised clinics nationwide, recognized by *Entrepreneur* magazine as one of the fastest growth franchise companies. I'm sorry to say that I don't think any of the others ever acted on their "big ideas." The difference between where Chris is now and where they are now has a lot less to do with the relative quality of their ideas than it does with the quantity of action.

In fact, enough action is almost irresistible to the marketplace, which I'll get to a bit later, in Section II of this book. That's an advanced secret.

One other story: Late in his life, I did some work with Joe Cossman, formally known as E. Joseph Cossman, and best known as the man who popularized the now iconic 1950s toy, The Ant Farm. Joe was a mail-order marketer who made ten different million dollar fortunes by finding ten different, existent, under-marketed products and bringing them to different avenues of distribution. He invented nothing. And, as he was the first to admit, he didn't do a thing anybody else couldn't do. As an example, he found a product, "fly cake," being manufactured and sold to the military, hospitals, and other institutions in bulk, to be put into buildings to trap and kill flies. He secured mail-order rights and sold it to homeowners, initially with small magazine and newspaper ads, then through countless catalogs. The manufacturer could have done it, but didn't—didn't experiment with any means of selling the product except the one method he started with.

The story of The Ant Farm is even more instructive. When Joe found it, its manufacturer was selling it only to schools, as a teaching aid for biology and earth-sciences classrooms. He recognized that kids would love to have this thing for themselves, and turned it into a blockbuster success as a toy. Joe told me he rarely went a week or two without hearing from a school teacher somewhere who said, "You know, I had the idea to do this before you did." I'm sure thousands of teachers did. None acted on their idea.

Getting into action on an idea is, itself, magnetic to opportunity and the resources needed to move it forward.

One day, while visiting my client, Greg Renker of the Guthy-Renker Corporation—then a fledgling direct marketing firm with a few TV infomercials under its belt, today a billion-dollar-a-year marketing conglomerate—he said, "I'd pay at least $10,000.00 to come to your office for a day, poke around in all your files and make copies of whatever interested me—you've probably got more samples of great ads, sales letters, and copy than anybody I know." By the time I got home, I'd toyed with the idea of holding days at my house when people came, paid, and got to attack all my files, but rejected it due to its obvious nuisance factor.

Instead I reasoned, if he'd pay $10,000.00, there are more who'd pay $1,000.00, and a lot more who'd pay a few hundred—if that experience was packaged and delivered. I narrowed the focus to all the marketing examples and information in my files about the sale of information—books, courses, seminars, and the like. The next day I wrote the first draft of the sales letter for a product, describing me dumping out all my files and photocopying the most interesting stuff and binding it together, and telling the story of the conversation with Greg as its genesis. Key words: the next day. You see, I got into motion, immediately.

A day or so later, I was having a phone conversation with Gary Halbert, mentioned earlier in this chapter, about my conversation with Greg Renker, the idea, the sales letter I'd started for the product-to-be, now called "The Ultimate Information Entrepreneur's Collection." He said his newsletter subscribers would love to get their hands on it, and offered to sell it to them, splitting revenues. Within a month, we sold over $200,000.00 worth. Another direct marketer with a big list of people interested in different kinds of business opportunities saw the mailing Gary and I did to his list, called me, asked to take it to his list, and the next month we sold over $100,000.00 worth of the big, ugly, clunky, photocopied manuals. This all before I even had a chance to sell it to my own customers! And this was some 25 years ago, when $300,000.00 was a good-sized chunk of change. This giant manual, slightly improved, lives on today (incidentally, available from Glazer-Kennedy Insider's Circle™ at DanKennedy.com). I suppose it's generated at least a few million dollars in its lifetime.

If space permitted, I could tell you another 20 very similar stories of my getting into motion with an idea and having the motion itself seem to attract the people, opportunity, resources, money needed to move forward. I said "seem" because I can't prove a concrete connection, but, personally, I don't believe in repetitive patterns of coincidence.

Bill Glazer owned two clothing stores in Baltimore, which he'd made fabulously successful with unusual and innovative marketing strategies based, in large part, on ideas he got from my books and courses. He sought me out when he saw I was coming to Baltimore and we had lunch. When he showed me what he was doing, I told him he should resell all his advertising and marketing to other clothing store owners, and I gave him a business plan to do so. It is a relatively formulaic approach to what I call the "niche information marketing business." Bill immediately began selling his "system" to other clothing store owners, then sporting goods retailers, then jewelers, then furniture store owners, and ultimately more than 10,000 independent retailers of every imaginable stripe, fueling a multi-million-dollar publishing business.

The plan he followed is one I've explained, shown, and taught, one way or another, to thousands of owners of all sorts of businesses. Quite a few others have used it to create great second businesses in information marketing—so many, in fact, there's an association of them, the Information Marketing Association, accessible at www.info-marketing.org. But . . . big, big but: For every one who has acted on this opportunity presented to them as Bill did, there are hundreds, if not thousands, who could have but didn't. They never got anywhere because they never got going and they never got going because they never got started.

Bill became such a master of this business that, about five years ago, I sold him mine, it became Glazer-Kennedy Insider's Circle™, and he now leads this multi-faceted publishing company serving a membership of more than 25,000 entrepreneurs worldwide. Bill has also achieved wide acclaim as an advertising guru, represented by his bestselling book, *Outrageous Advertising That's Outrageously Successful.*

All because he acted on an idea.

Do not err in focusing on the fact that none of the above examples have anything to do with the specific, particular business you are in. Consider only the behavioral commonality demonstrated in all of them. And take note of the side effect experienced by all of them.

I'll come at this two more ways. Mike Vance, a close associate of Walt Disney's for many years, consultant to top companies, and author of the book *Think Outside the Box*, tells the story of asking a troubled corporate CEO what his biggest, most vexing problem was. After he described it, Mike asked "Who's working on it?" The CEO said "No one." When Mike asked why, the CEO said, "Because it can't be solved." Against that, consider advice from General Norman Schwarzkopf. For three years, I followed General Schwarzkopf on seminar events, heard his speech so many times I memorized it without trying, and spent a lot of time in green rooms talking with him. One of the things that sticks in my mind is his contention that a bad decision or wrong decision is better than no decision, because if the decision leads to action, it is easier to correct the course of someone or something already in motion than it is to get someone or something into motion from inertia. In his groundbreaking work *"Psycho-Cybernetics,"* Dr. Maxwell Maltz presents "zig zagging" and "course correction" as the entire basis for human achievement; that hardly anybody gets to any goal via a straight line, but, instead, by moving, bumping up against something, moving a different way, bumping, zigging, zagging, but moving, moving, moving.

Finally, let me reveal one of my own, personal "secrets of success." It is a daily discipline I have adhered to for more than 30 years. I'd wager I've neglected it less than 30 days out of the 30 years, adhered to it 10,920 out of 10,950 days. Every day, no matter what else I am doing or must do that day, even if in a full day of consulting or traveling across country or on vacation, I still do one thing—if only one thing—intended to "prime my pump," to create future business for myself or my companies. It may be a small thing; tearing out a magazine article that should interest one of my clients, scrawling a note on it, and mailing it. It may be answering one item of correspondence. Getting one fax sent. Identifying a new, potentially useful contact, jotting a note, sending a book. But no day passes without me doing at least one such thing. Although it is no longer required, it has been especially important to me over the years because a lot of my income is derived from delivery of services, such as speaking, consulting, coaching, advertising copywriting, so, in a way, I must sell "it" and make "it." Most professionals stop selling while they're delivering, so they have dry spells, roller coaster ups and downs. I have had more demand than supply of me, and waiting lists of clients for many years because of my daily discipline of doing at least one proactive thing to attract business every single day.

WARNING
Highly Unflammable
You Might Not Catch on Fire from
Spontaneous Creative Combustion

(This'll scare a lot of people.)

"The biggest life lesson I learned is that you have to **discipline yourself to do the work.** If you want to accomplish something, you can't spend time hemming and hawing and making excuses. You actually have to do it. I still have to go home **every single day**, know where I am, what I'm doing—and include 45 minutes of practice on my clarinet, because I want to play. I want to write, too, so I get up, go in, close the door and write. You can't string paper clips and get a pad ready and play around."

—WOODY ALLEN

PUSH

"Incredible things happen
independently of those you personally create.
When you're pushing hard on Door A,
someone or something opens Door B.
Often, when you look through Door B,
what's behind it is much better than what
you were going after in the first place.
However, you wouldn't have seen Door B open
if you hadn't been in the hall pushing on Door A."

—JACK M. ZUFELT, AUTHOR, *THE DNA OF SUCCESS*,
WWW.DNAOFSUCCESS.COM

"Go through any open door.
If there is no door, make one."

—JOAN RIVERS

Wealth Magnet 11
Demonstration

Thomas Edison is known to most simply as a famous inventor, the man who provided us with the electricity in our homes and businesses, and sound recordings—before the iPod. But, although Edison was a prolific and successful inventor, in his time, by those in business, he was recognized as even more adept at demonstration than invention. To attract the almost endless number of private investors needed to fund his experiments, often extending over years without producing marketable product or income, Edison staged a series of heavily publicized, secret-until-the-moment "events" at which he spoke about and demonstrated the next amazing invention he was working on. Interestingly, Edison admitted often showing off ideas and projects he had no real intention of proceeding with, because the thing he really intended to fund did not lend itself well to simple explanation or to a mesmerizing, dramatic demonstration. (Later, he would switch the investor's stake from the faux project to the real one.) You may make what you will of his ethics, but you should learn from his commitment to Demonstration—even after his reputation was well-established.

Houdini made his reputation by visiting hundreds of police stations and jails, letting the police officers handcuff and imprison him with their own equipment, then escaping. Word spread, the news media soon became fascinated, and Houdini had made himself marketable by Demonstration. A modern comparable would be motivational guru and TV infomercial "giant," Tony Robbins, with whom I've appeared on seminar events a handful of times—Tony initially attracted media and public attention to himself with the "firewalk," a Demonstration of the power of the mental techniques he taught; he and his students walked barefoot along a trough of red hot coals. Never mind that famous fraud de-bunker Dr. James Randi has exposed this as a mere magic trick that proves nothing about mind-power, and magicians Penn and Teller have thoroughly exposed it as carnival trickery on their TV show *Bullshit* on Showtime. It brought Tony the attention he needed, and he still incorporates firewalks in his expensive, multi-day seminars today, although they have never been used in any of the TV infomercials about him produced and owned by my long-time client, the Guthy-Renker Corporation.

Today, of course, there's a great deal more media than when Edison was working to attract his investors or Houdini was wriggling out of police handcuffs and escaping jail cells in order to attract the public's attention. We're in a 24–7 news environment, with a gigantic media beast with voracious appetite for the next spectacle. There's also a lot of media you can directly control and use, at little or no cost, online—webinars, YouTube, Facebook, Twitter, etc. So a not-yet-famous chef or dog trainer or comedian or landscape designer or what-have-you can use Demonstration, to the public or to his own prospective clients or customers invited to "events" online, or use online media to invite them to actual events. Products can be demonstrated, virtual tours of properties provided, experiences presented for voyeuristic eavesdrop. Demonstration can be more easily done and disseminated than ever before. There's really no excuse anymore not to be utilizing Demonstration in context of publicity.

But there is more to this than the shrewd use of modern media, when you think in a broader sense of Demonstration as a Wealth Attraction Magnet. What Houdini understood and did so brilliantly was to make himself a 24/7 walking, talking, living Demonstration that was continuously attractive—not a video presentation turned on with the press of a button for a few minutes, then turned off and forgotten.

Another great example is David Ogilvy, profiled in the brilliant biography *The King of Madison Avenue*, which I urge you to read. As its title suggests, Ogilvy, a former short-order cook and door-to-door cookware salesman, made himself into the king of the advertising industry principally through Demonstration. (And, often, by creating exceptionally successful advertising.) When David Ogilvy secured the Rolls-Royce automobile account for his fledgling, up-and-coming ad agency, he immediately purchased a classic Rolls-Royce (that he couldn't really afford) to be driven about town in, park conspicuously outside his office building in New York, and ultimately be "caught in" and photographed by the media. He even procured a custom license plate: OMB2. The "OM" was for the agency name, Ogilvy & Mather; the "2" suggested the car might be the second Rolls-Royce in a fleet. It wasn't. Although the now legendary ad he created for Rolls-Royce was itself a dramatic demonstration of his ability, and was then much talked about in the ad industry and in other business circles, Ogilvy took care and went to extremes to make sure few missed the connection, Ogilvy and Rolls-Royce. Every drive to lunch or the corner store was Demonstration.

Think about Donald Trump, who I have also shared the platform with—as I have with his daughter, Ivanka Trump, his chief negotiator George Ross, and several *Apprentice* alumni. I've made quite a study of The Donald. It is my conviction that his penchant for plastering the TRUMP name all over everything, from building fronts to planes and his helicopter—seen zipping all over New York and New Jersey daily, and for licensing TRUMP as a brand for everything from bottled water to gourmet steaks sold on the home shopping channel QVC to his own how-to-get-rich books, is not ego. Or at least not *just* ego. Landing and exiting his helicopter emblazoned with his name, his private jet at the airport emblazoned with his name; dispensing instructions to *Apprentice* contestants with the Trump Tower emblazoned with his name behind him is all Demonstration of his importance, power, and success. A great many people want what Donald Trump has made himself a constant Demonstration of—success, power, and affluence. Luxury buyers want "the best of everything" that he stands for. Entrepreneurs want his success and wealth. This is the force that attracts them all to him, as viewers, book buyers and seminar attendees, consumers, hotel and resort guests, multi-million-dollar condominium buyers and real estate project partners and investors. His artful and strategic Demonstration is a wealth attraction force to be reckoned with.

Ogilvy, incidentally, once, tongue-in-cheek, threatened to sue a magazine over speculating about his being a genius rather than stating it. Trump has, in fact, sued at least one magazine for understating his wealth. There are quite a few other similarities between the two, so that I wonder if Trump studied Ogilvy— Trump is a serious student and voracious reader. But he need not have, as the behaviors used by the two to attract attention and interest and build reputation so as to attract wealth have been used and are used by many others for that same purpose.

While I was working on a draft of this chapter, Governor Sarah Palin, former vice-presidential candidate, did not quietly tender resignation from the governorship of Alaska with a letter, nor did she simply serve out her term but not seek re-election. She staged a sudden, unexpected, and dramatic announcement of her decision to leave office early on a Friday afternoon immediately before the July 4th weekend—a slow news period—in a picturesque setting outdoors, and delivered a passionate speech replete with quotable soundbites, drawing the nation's attention to her as if she was afire. If it hadn't been for Michael Jackson's death, she'd have been the #1 news story for several days. As it was, she was still the #1 political story, the person you saw when tuning in to any political TV talk show, and in the top five news stories for more than a week—during which time she reportedly concluded her book deal worth over $1-million, and began fielding a veritable flood of offers for paid speaking engagements, TV shows, even product endorsements. Her Demonstration relit a fading spotlight and reinforced her cultivated persona as an unpredictable, nontraditional political figure, self-styled maverick, and frank, plain-talking person that "regular folks" could identify with. What becomes of her as a political figure may or may not be known by the time you read these pages. But I'll wager, as I write these words, that she will have banked a great deal of money in the time lapsed between my writing this and you reading it.

There may be no one person who has ever attracted so much success and fame, and built such an amazing business on the strength of Personal Demonstration as Hugh Hefner. Hefner's iconic image, in smoking jacket; the Playboy Mansion; the publicized parties people nearly kill to gain admission to; most recently the three girlfriends are all Demonstration perfectly congruent with the reputation, brand, brand message, and motivations of the targeted consumers of Playboy.

This congruency is important and powerful.

I consider myself a thoughtful, thorough practitioner of such congruent Personal Demonstration. The better I've gotten at it, the more wealth has come to me. One of the key things I stand for, teach, and hold out as a prime benefit of understanding and using all my marketing, business development, and entrepreneurial success strategies is "autonomy"—meaning that you are the center of your universe, and you get to conduct business and live life entirely on your terms, doing business with whom you want, when you want, where you want, as you prefer. I've made almost every aspect of my life Demonstration of such autonomy.

In another book in this series, *No B.S. Time Management for Entrepreneurs*, I describe why and how I (and others adopting my methods) do not use e-mail or a cell phone, take no unscheduled incoming calls, work only by pre-set phone appointments, and achieve extraordinarily high productivity by working entirely protected from interruptions. I own and professionally drive harness racing horses, competing in over 150 races a year, and want to be available to drive at my home track every night there is racing. So after 15 years traveling extensively and speaking 70+ times a year, I radically re-arranged my business to stay home and compel consulting clients, coaching groups, mastermind groups, and even entire conferences to come to me. My consulting days, presently at fees upwards from $18,000.00, are conducted at my home—which is not that convenient for clients to travel to, being about an hour from a major airport and absent of taxi cabs. My days end at 4:00 P.M., so I have ample time to rest, eat, and get to the track to race. My own staff-person who runs my private office is at the opposite end of the country and we communicate by fax as needed, brief phone calls three times a week, and once a week I receive a well-organized box of in-bound faxes, mail, phone inquiries, etc., that have accumulated during the week, and to which I respond at my convenience. My own phone calls are all clumped into two days a month of back to back appointments, each for 10, 20, or 30 minutes with definite end times; clients and others may wait two to four weeks before getting to speak with me. In short, I am *famously* inaccessible, my time and productivity *famously* protected, everything in my business life *famously* arranged for my convenience. And for the record, it was like this long before I could afford it. It is all done for practical reasons but it is also dramatic Demonstration. And people get that. While some are annoyed and put off and do not do any business with me as a result, many more are attracted, fascinated, curious, envious, and want to know how they can create similar autonomy for themselves.

The way I work, the "rules" given to clients, the photos and videos of my racing shown at our websites and events and in my conference room, the classic cars I own and drive and show off, are Demonstration for me just as Trump's collection of Trump-labeled jets and helicopters and buildings are Demonstration for him.

In many respects, I think of myself as a "lifestyle brand," like Hugh Hefner or Martha Stewart. And make no mistake, Martha and Hef are much alike in profitable use of Demonstration. In her television show and magazine, we see her homes, gardens, kitchen, and we get the sense that she lives what she espouses—and then hope we can get the same sort of elegance and artistry in our homes and lives by buying the products bearing her name. She is Personal Demonstration and her life is Demonstration. I, too, have media, although certainly not as far-reaching as hers; mine consists of a portfolio of newsletters read by my customers, online media read and viewed by our customers, and my appearances at events. Through those media I strive to convey a consistent, congruent Demonstration of the beneficial outcomes of adopting my strategies and philosophies, which people connect to by buying the books, courses, business tools, and other products bearing my name. Every story I tell, experience I share, activity I "show off"; the look inside my life and my living of it, is Demonstration. In my case, it has the added value of authenticity.

There is a burden to it, by the way. I have to restrict myself from incongruent actions. Even if there's a free shuttle bus to take me from a hotel a short distance to a convention center, I can't be seen riding it; I *must* arrive in luxury sedan, driven by a chauffer. Even if I am tempted to immediately jump on the phone and return a call to someone who has inquired about making a deal, someone I'm eager to do business with, I can't. I must let our process do its work; I must have my assistant schedule a phone appointment. I can't do such things any more than diet and exercise guru Richard Simmons dare be seen at McDonalds wolfing down a Big Mac and a super-sized mountain of fries or Martha Stewart be seen at the mall in cheap sweat pants with stains on them and dirty sneakers. Even if Donald Trump found mowing the grass relaxing and therapeutic, he dare not be seen out there in shorts and a T-shirt, pushing the mower at Mar-A-Lago. He *needs* to be on the golf course, with celebrities or business leaders, wearing perfectly cleaned and pressed sportswear.

Warren Buffett has cultivated the image of a simple, small town, not-Wall Street, folksy sage, who lives in a modest home bought many years ago, who prefers his neighborhood restaurant, and drinks Coca-Cola® just like "regular folk." So he worried quite a bit about the incongruency of finally buying his own jet, appropriately named *The Indefensible*, and was relieved to replace it with NetJets' service—after buying the company. Buffett is not eager to have his other luxury homes publicized, nor, when his wife was alive, have simultaneous existence of his official wife living apart and seen at certain social and business functions and his unofficial, at-home-in-Omaha second wife publicized either. For good reason: gross incongruency with his popular Personal Demonstration of a heartland-of-America, common sense, classic values guy, your wise uncle, stable and steadfast and, above all else, as trustworthy as the daily rising of the sun. Of course, given his wealth and status, he could afford the risk of such incongruities, but he has nevertheless been mindful of them, and has taken pains to minimize their public visibility. I recommend reading the comprehensive biography of Buffett, *Snowball*.

You may think you are not a "lifestyle brand" like Hefner or Buffett or Martha or me, but why not? If you are a financial advisor or investment broker, what should you be representing by your own Personal Demonstration? Presumably affluence and financial security, perhaps autonomy. If you are a doctor, shouldn't you be a Demonstration of good health and the virtues of healthy living habits and disciplines? Whatever it is that you sell or otherwise exchange for money, there is some sort of Personal Demonstration for it.

So, for you, the questions have to do with how good a Demonstration you are for what you stand for, symbolize, and promise to your particular constituency of customers, clients, or investors. Are you a walking, talking, living, obvious and clear Personal Demonstration? Is your Personal Demonstration congruent? Could you strengthen your Personal Demonstration?

Congruent Personal Demonstration is very, very magnetic.

And *the* Playboy® bunny keeps going and going and going . . .

A demonstration of Demonstration

The following two articles are reprinted from *RENEGADE MILLION-AIRE* magazine, Vol. 1, Issue 4 (Fall/Winter '08), from www.Renegade Millionaire.com. They are based, in part, on Hef's *Little Black Book* by Hugh M. Hefner with Bill Zehme, published by Harper-Collins; articles in *Playboy* magazine; and other biographical sources. PLAYBOY is a registered trademark of Playboy Enterprises Inc.

"Gentlemen, gentlemen,
be of good cheer,
for they are out there
and we are in here!"

The official Playboy Mansion toast created by
actor Robert Culp (*I Spy*)

Lessons in Marketing
The Making and Marketing of PLAYBOY Is Not as Simple as it Would Seem

How hard is it to sell sex? A magazine filled with pictures of naked women? Such a simplistic view would have Disney in the amusement park business, Starbucks in the coffee business, Victoria's Secret in the underwear business, and NetJets in the transportation business.

From the beginning, the magazine was about much more than bared breasts. It celebrated materialism, living the good life, and being an independent thinker, even a rebel, in rejecting society's critical judgments and traditional "rules" in favor of your own path. At a point, frustrated by having this overlooked, Hefner began writing about "The Playboy Philosophy," beginning with a series of essays extending over many months' issues of the magazine. It was this Philosophy, enunciated, illustrated, and demonstrated that defined the relationship between the majority of the magazine's readers and Hefner and his magazine. They may have been attracted at first by the buxom babes, but quickly discovered there was more at stake. *Playboy* is based on a profound "sense of place" where men feel understood, welcome, and encouraged to never quite grow up. To further this, Hefner created a concept for full-page ads in his own magazine addressing his own readers, headlined "What Sort of a Man Reads *Playboy*?" in which he presented a profile worthy of aspiration. These ads continue today.

Playboy is the ultimate example of symbolism. Hef's robe and pipe are to him what a hat was for Sinatra or drink in hand for Dean Martin; the Mansion, the imagination-stoking representation of the Lifestyle To Aspire To. The bunny trademark, consistently one of the top five most recognized symbols the world over, in company with the Coca-Cola logo and Mickey Mouse. The pipe, incidentally, was deliberately chosen, inspired, Hef admits, by the dashing hero Pat Ryan in the *Terry and the Pirates* comic strip of his youth, and by Sherlock Holmes.

Hefner originally called his magazine *Stag Party*, and had designed a logo of an antlered buck swilling a cocktail—but a cease-and-desist letter from lawyers representing an existent "skin" magazine called *Stag* ended that. The tuxedoed bunny, a symbol of the constant pro-creation in the animal kingdom, later adapted by a battery company for similar symbolism, was his second choice. This, too, reveals something casual observers seldom realize about the huge successes around them; that they were not built methodically from the ground up, as if a house from an architect's blueprint, nor achieved in a straight line; they represent achievement overcoming unanticipated obstacles, the achiever dodging and weaving and bumbling down blind alleys and reversing, falling, and failing and getting up and re-starting. (In another Disney similarity, Walt began with Oswald the Rabbit, and on turning to the mouse, named him Mortimer, switch-ing to the friendlier Mickey only under pressure from his wife.)

Playboy has nearly fallen by the wayside as antiquated—even too quaint in a massively sexed media world—at two different times, but proven a brand that cannot die. In its current renaissance, the first of the new Playboy Clubs is open and thriving atop the trendy Palms resort in Las Vegas with two others set to open; the magazine is alive and well, inter-linked with a cable TV network, a film-to-DVD publish-ing business, catalog and e-commerce businesses, a monster-sized brand licensing business placing the rabbit head, the Playboy bunnies in their famous costume, and even Hef on thousands of different prod-ucts, and a popular cable-TV reality show with a second in the works.

And he keeps going and going and going and going . . .

HUGH HEFNER,
THE PLAYBOY EMPIRE,
AND A TRIBUTE TO THE MAGIC OF THINKING BIG!

"And so one man created two houses and all men would forever want to go to these houses, to be inside." This is how biographer Bill Zehme described Hugh Hefner's Playboy Mansions—the original, set up in Chicago in 1959, and the current Los Angeles mansion, seen weekly in the E network's reality show about Hefner's life, *The Girls Next Door*. The existential importance of Hef's Mansion was shown off in a *Playboy* magazine cartoon, circa 1970, in which a man has clambered to a mountain peak to beg wisdom from a guru. The wise man at the top of the mountain tells the man: "There's a man who lives in a mansion full of beautiful women and wears pajamas all the time. Sit at his feet and learn from him, for he has found the secret of true happiness." The Mansion, the mystery about what goes on there, and Hef himself, are beautifully crafted symbols of a lifestyle and attitude on which a far-flung, flourishing empire has been built, now, maybe ironically, run by a woman, his daughter.

It would be a mistake to think of Hefner as a mere playboy, though. Ever. He has lived a life as a workaholic, and one of the main reasons for the establishment of that first Playboy Mansion was to eliminate a commute from home to office to home. To as great an extreme as any highly successful entrepreneur, Hefner so blurred the lines between his work and play, work life and personal life, they are discernible only to him. With clear commonality with mega-entrepreneurs like Walt Disney, Donald Trump, Richard Branson, Vince McMahon (profiled in the last issue of this magazine), Hefner has been a creative and relent-less self-promoter, in that way also blurring line between business and personal. As an aside, Disney was developing his outside-the-box empire in the same time frame as was Hefner. One has to assume they watched each other with interest—and borrowed from each other liberally. Walt had Mickey, Minnie, then Donald and Pluto; Hef had his bunnies; each their own version of the happiest place on earth.

Like all other Renegade Millionaires, Hefner defied work norms. At his peak, when personally doing or supervising just about everything in the magazine, about the magazine, and about the business developing around it, he explained, "I don't take calls anymore; I only return them at my convenience. I do not go to people; people come to me. I don't even need to dress; I just put on a robe. I have discovered I don't have to arrange my life by other people's hours." Hef was famous for disappearing from his own parties into his private quarters, to his giant bed used as giant desk, strewn on one side with magazine layouts, articles, photos, and corporate reports, space preserved on the other side for "personal activity." He tended to sleep a lot during the day then combine work and play all through the evening, night, and into the wee hours—observing that "all the best things happen at night." While the details may differ slightly, Hefner shared in common with most other Renegade Millionaires the oft-criticized and, to so many, puzzling determination of making the entire world revolve around him. Today, his pace has slowed, his work hours lessened, more responsibilities delegated, yet he is still actively engaged in business every day, and still the chief symbol and promoter of *Playboy* to its generations of fans and customers—and still apt to mix a dinner with friends, movie in the Mansion's theater, a poker game with friends, disappearing several times to work, and disappearing a time or two for other activities, all into one marathon evening.

Hefner began his magazine with nearly zero resources, but for—appropriately in this case—brass balls. As example, his confession: "I had two different letterheads—one for the magazine, the other for my imaginary distributing company called Nationwide News Company. When I wrote a letter on the magazine's stationery, I was the editor, publisher, or promotion, advertising, or circulation director, as circumstances dictated. When I was writing to news-dealers, I was the general manager or president of Nationwide News Company. I was the entire staff of both. That's all there was—just me, my typewriter, and a card table."

His troubles with getting his magazine printed and distributed disappeared thanks to Marilyn Monroe—and more of Hefner's chutzpah. Two nude photos of Marilyn were discovered, but *Life* magazine printed only one—small, and black and white. No other magazines would touch them, and only one was produced in a calendar. Hefner went to the calendar company that owned the photos, walked in "cold," and negotiated permission to use the other photo for $500.00. The Marilyn cover of *Playboy* quickly produced 70,000 advance orders and a distribution contract with the #1 magazine distributor. The "big break," too often called a "lucky break," is common to the Renegade Millionaire experience, usually occurring more than once, at essential moments. As in Hefner's case, the big break is typically created through bold action, in many cases attempting something that would, on the surface, seem impossible.

Some 54 years ago, or so, Hugh Hefner began his epic entrepreneurial journey, turning a simple idea into a sprawling global empire and himself into an icon, all powered by self-belief, self-promotion, and the selling of aspirations. Of course it didn't hurt that sex was involved. Psychologists claim sex is on the minds of most, more often than anything else. But this great American success story is about much more than that. And Hefner stands as a living tribute to the incredible power of thinking big—and acting on one's thoughts.

Wealth Magnet 12
Follow-Up

A lot of people never start. Never do anything. Then, of those who do start, few follow through.

A lot of business owners, marketers, and sales professionals who start promising and creating valuable relationships with prospects, customers, or clients never follow up to develop them and sustain them. This is not just a matter of disorganization, dysfunction, or sloth. It has deeper meaning.

My experience with entrepreneurs constantly enjoying a massive and steady flow of customers or clients, opportunities, and wealth streaming to them is that they think in terms of "process" rather than "incident," and "opportunity" rather than "outcome," and I teach them to think in these terms.

Beware the Gold Star Syndrome

There is a little lecture I always give to my peers who are professional speakers about The Gold Star Syndrome. I'll bring it to you in a minute. But first, here's what happens when most speakers get a booking. Let's say someone's asked to speak on October 7th for the International Hardware Retailers Association. The speaker hangs up the phone, pumps the air with celebratory fist, gets a file folder and writes Hardware Retailers Association on it and files it, goes over to the big calendar on the wall and sticks a big gold star on the October 7 square and writes IHRA on the star with a marker. Then he runs up the stairs from his basement office to tell his wife, and they go out to dinner and have steak and lobster to celebrate.

This displays the fundamental misunderstanding of speaking as a business (which it isn't) that keeps most speakers living gig to gig, paycheck to paycheck, as well as **most business owners' fundamental misunderstanding of what making a sale to a new customer is**, which keeps most of them broke, too.

In reality, there's nothing here to celebrate (yet), anymore than there would be if the garden center delivered and dumped a huge truckload of manure in your backyard at the edge of your garden. **It's the _start_ of the work to be done, not an end result or outcome.** If you think of it as an end result, your garden would never flourish and you'd arrive at harvest time with nothing but a giant pile of rotting, stinking dung attracting flies.

In speaking, when I put the gold star on a square on my calendar—and I did, for many years 40 to 70 times a year in addition to the 27 SUCCESS-event appearances each year, for a total of more than 1,500 compensated engagements during my stint* at it. The engagement's included plenty of Iowa and Arkansas and Florida State Associations of this or that, and corporations like

---

*I am by choice nearly retired from speaking outside of Glazer-Kennedy Insider's Circle™. I take only a few extra engagements a year, most of the time requiring the client to put them in one of my home towns.

Honda, Pitney-Bowes, IBM, and franchise and sales organizations like Floor Coverings International and Sun Securities—it was the same as the starting gun firing; it was the start of a race to engineer as many ways and means and contributing factors as possible between then and the engagement date, to optimize the money made at and after the date. You need not be bored with the specific details, but there is a checklist of 20 smart questions to ask and things to do. A complex process to implement and manage.

In every business, the same thing is true, the same opportunity exists and is, mostly, wasted. Someone calls and makes a reservation at your restaurant—the Gold Star Syndrome occurs. Of course, you could check your file on the customer and have the assigned waitperson read the customer profile so they could ask about their dog, tell them the chef has prepared their favorite appetizer. If a new, first-time customer, you could Google® them to see if they are prominent or special or a potentially valuable center of influence. You could immediately FedEx them a special voucher to add two to four friends to their dinner party that night and receive a free bottle of wine for the table. Etc., etc. In every business, the same thing is true—the acquisition of a new customer is seen as a means of making a sale, and as an outcome . . . not the starting point of a process. This reflects focus only on Present Bank, not Future Bank, of course, but it goes beyond and deeper than that, into **your view of what kind of business you are in.** To use the restaurant owner, is he in the business of selling and serving food? Or of acquiring and *developing* VIP customers with whom he has strong relationships, and developing and mining maximum equity in those assets? Another way to think about it is—where should the first gold star be awarded? Certainly not in advance of an actual event. Almost certainly not with the first transaction. There should be better benchmarks of effectiveness and success.

Bring it all the way down to the simplest of situations. Your own daily life. When you go and dine at a restaurant for the first time, get clothes cleaned at a dry cleaners for the first time, go

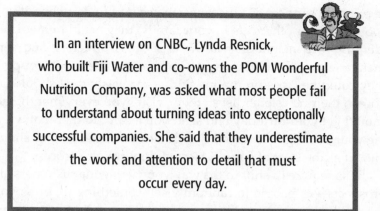

In an interview on CNBC, Lynda Resnick, who built Fiji Water and co-owns the POM Wonderful Nutrition Company, was asked what most people fail to understand about turning ideas into exceptionally successful companies. She said that they underestimate the work and attention to detail that must occur every day.

into a different shop of one kind or another for the first time—of the many, many times you do this, how many times have you immediately gotten a follow-up letter from the restaurant or shop owner thanking you for coming in and inviting you back? How many have sent you an interesting newsletter every month afterward, to create and maintain a presence with you? The answer will be: hardly any. Or: none. Your entering and departing their place of business is an "outcome" to them. To me, the person coming in for the very first time is a magnificent "opportunity." The way you view it will determine what you do about it. Few businesses have any set means of identifying first-time customers, of getting their contact information to follow up. Even fewer do follow up. But I assure you, those few who do prosper as a result.

Now let's talk about "process" versus "incident."

To take this to an "ordinary" business, consider the quick-oil-change shop in your neighborhood. They probably have a process in place to do "upsells"—additional things you need, like a new oil filter. They probably capture your contact information and send you a reminder postcard when it's about time for your next oil change. But that's it, and there's so much more they could do. For example, they could try to sell you a coupon book of pre-paid services at a discount; they could find out about your spouse's car or other cars in your family; they could immediately identify your neighbors via the criss-cross directory and send them a letter noting you were a happy customer, with coupons; they could be cross-promoting with a car wash; they should put you on their newsletter list so they "visit" you every month; they should get your birthday and send you a card. Rather than viewing your coming in for an oil change as an "incident," they should view it as the start of a multi-faceted, continuing "process."

This requires a shift in the way you view your customers and prospects—as people to randomly sell something to, or as your most valuable assets, to build and maintain a solid fence around, to care for, coddle, develop strong relationships with, and multiply through referrals. Selling things to people makes money. Developing and owning assets creates wealth. You have to decide what you're about.

Why Is Follow Up So Magnetic?

Wealth and rarity go together. The rarer the art, the piece of jewelry, the designer gown, the travel experience, the first edition book, the celebrity's autograph, the professional expertise, the higher the price paid, the greater the appreciation, the greater the demand.

Many people in many businesses tell me theirs is an ordinary or, worse, commoditized business where rarity and exclusivity just don't apply. This reflects poverty of imagination, very much linked to financial poverty. Consider Disney for a moment. Their parks are open to and for the masses, and offer no rarity other than excellence. But there are different types of Disney hotels and resorts, from modestly priced to pricey and unique, like Animal Kingdom Lodge. There, if you pay the premium for a savannah-view room, wild animals roam nearly within an ¡arm's length of your balcony. Walk out and look a giraffe in the eye. If you stay on the concierge level—and only if you stay there—you can go on a backstage Safari at Dawn. If you wish, for about $125.00 an hour, you can hire your own personal guide to escort you through the parks. For a fee, your family can have a private lunch with a Disney Imagineer. If you own a time-share in the Vacation Club, there are lodgings with abundant numbers of suites but there are also a small number of tree houses. Disney creates tiers of exclusivity and rarity.

But let's assume for sake of argument that such examples fall on deaf ears, and you devoutly and stubbornly believe there's nothing whatsoever about your products, services, expertise, or business rarer than rocks in the quarry; certainly not as rare as the Crown Jewels. There is still one rarity you can create and own, the rarest of attributes that is extremely attractive and magnetic to wealth precisely because of its rarity: diligent, fail-safe follow up. That can be installed in *any* business.

Wealth Magnet 13
Integrity

R elax. I'm not about to deliver a morality lecture. In fact, we can forget all about the very idea of morality for this discussion. We can simply be pragmatic.

Pragmatism basically means doing what best serves your interests. Doing what delivers the results you desire. Doing what works.

You need not think in terms of doing what's right at all.

Let's just talk about doing the right things as pragmatists. Not what's right morally. What's right pragmatically.

The number-one complaint everybody has about the people and companies they do business with, buy from, get mad at, and stop buying from is: The vendor doesn't keep his promises.

I've had quite a few lawyers in my private coaching groups. It's not by design! I try to discourage them, but there they are.

And they've confirmed for me as fact: the number one reason lawyers lose clients AND the number one cause of complaints about lawyers to the bar association is not incompetence or malpractice, not overcharging, not failure—it is merely and simply not communicating with clients. In the printing industry, where I've owned businesses, have and had clients, done a lot of work, and spent millions myself, the number one reason that clients fire printers and go elsewhere is: missed deadlines. In the restaurant industry, the number one reason that companies stop ordering for delivery from a particular restaurant is: late delivery.

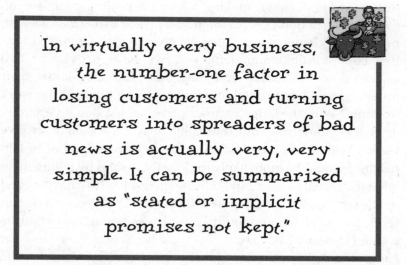

> In virtually every business, the number-one factor in losing customers and turning customers into spreaders of bad news is actually very, very simple. It can be summarized as "stated or implicit promises not kept."

Conversely, one of the biggest Wealth Attractants ever invented is simply saying what you will do and doing what you say. When you become known for absolute reliability, customers, clients, opportunity, and money will flow to you in ever-increasing abundance. The word spreads because you are so rare. Price competition becomes irrelevant.

Like everyone else, I occasionally get myself into a situation where I can't meet a deadline, can't keep a promise. I am maniacal about not letting this happen, and take every commitment, from simple punctuality to the more complex seriously, so the operable word is "occasionally." It makes me nuts when it does happen because, as a pragmatist, I know how detrimental to my interests it is. When it does occur, I've learned not to run and hide or ignore it and hope it goes unnoticed, but to confront it, to apologize, and to make it right. Again, not out of ethical or moral obligation but out of pragmatism; choosing the best business strategy.

And here's something rather "advanced," that very few entrepreneurs ever discover: A less appealing promise kept serves you better than making a more appealing promise you can't, won't, or don't keep. I often find myself in discussions with prospective clients, where I may be given a high-fee, very lucrative copywriting assignment, and we have arrived at two issues—potential results and time; how can they know their investment will be profitable? How soon can they get the work from me? With the latter, naturally, they would like it yesterday or at least tomorrow, but the reality may be six, eight, twelve weeks. With the first issue, they'd like to be reassured of certain results. I would be more likely to close these sales by telling them what they want to hear, but I'd be much less likely to have a good relationship with that client over time. And I believe, on a certain level, the other fellow would know I was telling him what he wanted to hear. I say: *I know what you'd like to hear about speed, but I am not going to make you promises I can't keep.* I say: *I want you to remember there are no guarantees here, other than my best efforts bringing all my experience to bear. I do fail. I might fail with your project.* This way I get their respect, not just a sale.

The New Economy is a place where free, almost wild spending has been replaced with more limited, discriminate spending. There is a new insistence on reliability and trustworthiness. The yearning in consumers, investors, and businesspeople involved with other businesspeople is for authenticity, integrity, and reliability—not anxiety.

Wealth Magnet 14
Ask

This is even Biblical. Ask and ye shall receive.

And everybody knows it. You don't ask, you don't get. Yet a whole lot of people who know it don't actually practice it much. They go through life wanting all sorts of things they never seem to work up the courage to ask for. So they're unhappy in their business because they don't ask their clients, vendors and employees. They're unhappy in their marriage because they don't ask their spouse. By 'ask', I mean a composite of things. Clearly enunciating your desires, expectations and, when appropriate, demands. Asking people to do things as you want them done. Seeking co-operation and support.

Even fewer people ask "outsiders."

I've found that it's perfectly okay to ask for a lot from a lot of people. I ask people for information, advice, ideas, contacts and

"I Want It All.
And I Want It Delivered."

—MAGNET ON MY REFRIGERATOR

introductions, and all sorts of assistance, pretty much with impunity. I am also generous with reciprocity and reward. But I ask.

Just for example, I have had more than 250 different people involved in the initial promotion for the book you are reading and the other books in the No B.S. series. I got this publisher to do things they have not done for any other author (which they'd prefer I didn't mention). I got famous and not-so-famous authors and speakers to send e-mails to their lists, "plug" the books in their speeches and newsletters, put information about the books up on their websites. I received more than 2.5 million (!) e-mails at zero cost. I got people to pay to host promotional events and tele-seminars. On and on and on. Mostly because I asked. Did I get everybody I asked to participate? No. But I got a whole lot more people to participate than if I hadn't asked anybody. Did I get everybody to do everything I wanted them to do? No. But I got a lot more than if I hadn't asked.

I know a few other authors who are great askers. My friend, Mark Victor Hansen, co-creator of the publishing phenomenon, the *Chicken Soup for the Soul* series, is a phenomenal asker. If he meets a celebrity, king, president, athlete, CEO, anybody and everybody, he asks them for something, to somehow help him promote himself or his books or his causes, to introduce him to somebody else he wants to meet. You might think such asking, asking, asking would repel people and wind up with you standing alone as if you had body odor, but the opposite occurs. The asking is magnetic. Actually people, especially successful people, like being asked for their ideas, opinions, and advice, like being asked for their help and influence. Often, you even get more than you ask for! There's another author who called up Trump's office "cold" and asked to have The Donald look at his book manuscript and give him a quote. Trump gave him a quote and an entire extra chapter to add to the book, a lot of marketing muscle for the book.

With that in mind, I'd like to ask YOU to promote this book. Go to www.NoBSBooks.com and click on "viral." There, you'll find some ready-to-use e-mails you can forward, free articles you can copy and send, all sorts of nifty goodies you can give to your entrepreneur friends. And if you happen to be an association executive or corporate big dog or somebody else with a big list of businesspeople who know you and respect you, I'd be happy to hear from you personally, and we can figure out something—maybe a special free tele-seminar you gift to everybody, for example. I'm game. Send me a fax with some details at 602-269-3113. (Please be patient. It might be two to three weeks before I can respond.)

See, I asked.

Of course, it helps to be able to give to get, sometimes in advance of the asking, or least reciprocate to get, and to offer reciprocation. It's not essential, but it is helpful. If you're really, really perceptive you'll realize how I've used this book, done things within this book, to support my asking for assistance promoting the book. If you figure it out, it's a secret not limited to authors and books. Any business owner could use the same strategy. Every business owner has media: customer newsletter, bags and box lids, in-store signage, window displays, and more. Every business owner has basis for co-operating with others.

Wealth is more readily attracted through co-operation than independent action. Strategic alliances are the new world order in The New Economy. As costs of acquisition—of leads, of customers, of information, of resources—have risen, sharing of those assets and resources has grown evermore important. Timidity about proposing such alliances imposes severe handicap. I have improved my bank balance a great deal, often, with conversations I initiate, beginning with "You know, we should do *something* together."

Wealth Magnet 15
Domino Opportunity

A lot of entrepreneurs get gifted with a lot of opportunity. It's just not lack or shortage of opportunity that explains anybody's lack of wealth.

Phil McGraw was a family therapist who disliked private practice, dabbled in speaking, the personal growth seminar business, corporate consulting on human resources matters, and even consulting with lawyers on jury selection and witness preparation. He was handed the gift of consulting with the lawyers hired to defend Oprah Winfrey when she was sued over her negative remarks about beef. Lots of consultants would have collected a fat fee and an autographed photo and been happy to get them, and that would be that. Dr. Phil became Dr. Phil by dominoing that opportunity.

You may never get such a giant and obvious opportunity. But you most certainly do get many opportunities, day in, day out, that you fail to domino.

As a personal example, a trade journal for attorneys, *Pennsylvania Lawyer,* published a chapter from my *No B.S. Time Management* book as an article. I immediately went into the domino-the-opportunity mode: A copy of article and book sent to the other 49 states' law journals, to try and get published, to promote my books, in those magazines; a copy of the article to several clients who market to lawyers, run seminars for lawyers, etc., with encouragement to reprint the article and distribute it to their customers. Sure, it's a small thing. But you sell 50,000 books one book at a time. So it's all about small things multiplied, as is most marketing and promotion. So one article dominoed into 5 or 8 or 20 is a small thing multiplied equaling a big thing. Often, when one of my books is released, we organize a teleseminar with me, or an online video program with me, and typically get from 5,000 to 15,000 people to attend. We create that opportunity and leverage it with a vast network of other authors, publishers, business coaches, and consultants and others, so that the 5,000 comes from 500 sources. More importantly, we domino this opportunity before, during, and after, with a complex, multi-step, multi-media marketing campaign for the book and for membership in Glazer-Kennedy Insider's Circle™.

This is an attitude, an approach that those adept at wealth attraction cultivate in themselves, so the domino-opportunity behavior becomes second nature, so every opportunity gets dominoed. It's also something that feeds on itself, as one opportunity dominoed tends to bring other opportunities. Momentum occurs. This is why Ken Kragen, a master publicist and promoter, who launched a number of entertainers' careers, including Kenny Rogers, always strived to create a chain of three linked events occurring in quick succession, rather than one publicity event; to go beyond getting attention, and creating momentum.

Just as it is more difficult to attract customers in The New Economy, as they strive to be more thoughtful and prudent about their spending, it is harder than ever to get attention and hold it for any length of time. A media environment once made up of three TV networks, evening news, newspapers, and a few weekly magazines has first, fragmented with hundreds of cable stations and 24/7 news and news-talk, then second, exploded online with thousands of options, blogs, websites, YouTube, Facebook, and on and on. Migration occurs backwards from new media to old media. One of the weeks I was working on this chapter, a homemade video of a wedding bride and escort and entire group of family and friends dancing down the aisle to hip-hop music made its way to YouTube, and from there to cable and network TV, its participants twice brought "live" to the *Today Show,* and it topped five-million viewers on YouTube—but it was over, gone, and forgotten in five days. If it had been fabricated for commercial purposes, the means of dominoing the opportunity existed. But if the entrepreneur didn't have a plan and didn't act decisively, quickly, and expansively to domino that opportunity, it would be wasted. Domino or disappear, that's the way it is these days.

Wealth Magnet 16
Passion

There's a *whole lot of metaphysical foolishness*, in books, CDs, seminars, pushing the simplistic premise: do what you love to do and money will follow. Now there is a giant, steaming, stinking pile of b.s.! Sure, happy accidents happen, but do you want to wager your future on freak incidents?

I like to lie in a hammock. I like to read. Eat pizza. Watch football. I have yet to figure out how to get people to line up and pay to watch me do that. Doesn't matter how much I enjoy those things. My enjoyment can multiply, the money won't.

This idea that you can do what you like, or feel most passionately about and be assured of attracting wealth is silly and childish. Appealing, certainly. But silly and childish. At some point we must outgrow childish things. One of my earliest mentors taught me that maturity meant, in part, that you stopped letting your "wants" control you. In fact, our wants are often in conflict and some must be given priority over others. I have a passionate love for carb-loaded Mexican food, including "junk" Mexican food from Taco Bell, but I am a non-insulin-dependent diabetic, I control my disease with diet, nutritional supplements, and fitness, and I have a passionate interest in driving professionally in harness races, which requires me to have my diabetes under control, and I have a strong interest in a long life, too. Mature choices must be made. Same principle applies to attracting wealth. If you indulge wants in conflict with wealth attraction, you trade away wealth for fulfillment of those wants.

If you don't get it through inheritance, marrying into it, or random luck, most wealth comes through businesses, and businesses must be market driven. *Not* personal joy driven. Market driven. The list of people who got out of bed this morning hoping *you* will have passion and joy today is probably short. But the lists of people who get out of bed in the morning with diseases they desperately want cures for, problems they urgently seek solutions for, hopes and dreams they need help fulfilling, conveniences they'd welcome if offered—those lists are long. If you want to attract maximum wealth with minimum effort in minimum time, here's the formula: find such a list for which you can engineer your own superior answer.

You *do* want to avoid drudgery. No one can maintain self-motivation and productivity very long when engaged in activities they find mind-numbing or onerous, or dealing with people they despise, or doing work they find unfulfilling, or selling things they do not believe in. This is a certain path to poverty. But, on the other hand, only doing what you like with no regard to market demand is just as certain a path to poverty.

Truth is, you rarely get all the results you want only from activities and processes you prefer. Maturity involves opting for desirable results rather than pleasing activities.

There's also a popular metaphysical idea—don't pursue money, pursue passion. Pfui. I'm a writer, and I like Mark Twain's quote: "No one but a blockhead writes but for money." I hear people say they like their work so much they'd do it even if they weren't being paid. I think that's frightening and dangerous. Someone in business needs to think in a businesslike way. Why would I write just to write? I write for an audience who will pay money. Otherwise, it's like being the tree that falls in the distant, unpopulated forest, heard or noticed by no one. What's the point?

So, let's try re-arranging some items. In no particular order:

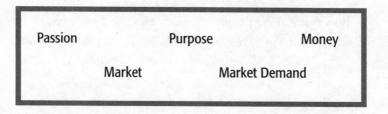

| Passion | Purpose | Money |
| Market | Market Demand | |

The very unbusinesslike arrangement would be: passion, purpose, market, market demand, money. Pursue your passion, indulge your purpose or mission with no regard for a market or market demand, and hope to attract wealth. I again say to you: Hope is not a strategy.

The business arrangement would be: market, market demand, purpose, passion, money. Identify a viable, preferably under-served market, determine market demand (what it wants most and will pay for), then align your purpose, and do something for the market that you can feel passionately about.

A Passion for Wealth

". . . the claim that people did not set out to get rich, but became rich by 'accident'—'Oh, I just did what I love to do and woke up one day to find myself wealthy.'

. . . the vast majority of the self-made rich worked, secretly or openly, deliberately, intentionally, like billy-o to acquire wealth."

". . . and now look around you. How many of the people you work with, the people you socialize with, the people you see in the street, do you think have DEDICATED THEMSELVES to getting rich?"

—FELIX DENNIS, ONE OF BRITAIN'S WEALTHIEST ENTREPRENEURS, CREATOR OF *MAXIM* MAGAZINE, AND AUTHOR OF *HOW TO GET RICH*

Wealth Magnet 17
See What Isn't There

Way back in 1982, I started a company from scratch, with less than $1,000.00, that produced millions of dollars over the next several years, and attracted customers who continue contributing to my income today, all these years later. It was classic entrepreneurial alchemy—nothing but an idea on a Monday, $100,000.00 in income by the following Friday. Before the internet, incidentally. At the risk of distracting you from the point, I'll give you the specifics, but with the warning to focus on the principle.

At the time, in the chiropractic profession, information and advice about practice marketing, promotion, and success was being delivered to doctors at two price levels: very inexpensive books and audiocassette tapes, priced at $10.00 to $100.00, or multi-year practice management programs, costing upwards of

$25,000.00. There was nothing in between. Further, the way practice management was sold was via small, free introductory seminars, city by city by city. As a result, 30 or 40 doctors in a town would attend, eager for help, but only one might be willing to make the required investment. *The business I created stepped into the gap, the empty market space in the middle.* We followed the practice management companies, again put those 30 or 40 doctors into a seminar, but offered them a $300.00 to $500.00 alternative. Virtually 100% bought. In 36 months, more than 10,000 of only 35,000 eligible chiropractors in the entire profession bought one or more of our courses—an amazing 30% market share. Now, forget all about chiropractors and seminars and courses. Focus on stepping into the empty or underserved market space.

When a client of mine created Steak 'n Ale restaurants, there were a lot of premium steakhouses, like Ruth Chris' and Morton's, and a lot of very low-end steakhouses, like Sizzler, but hardly anything in between. He developed a restaurant that combined the ambience, feel, and quality of a premium steakhouse with pricing in between the two extremes. He benefited from a recession. And he got very rich.

For years, air travel options were fly commercial, coach, or first class, charter a private plane, or own a jet. A few companies, notably including NetJets, in which Warren Buffett is invested, found market space in the middle. Bringing the time sharing and fractional ownership formats from real estate, they created fractional jet ownership. Many celebrities as well as CEOs, executives, and entrepreneurs are "owners"/clients of these companies. Famous names you know, like Martha Stewart, and lots of people you don't know too. And those companies were well positioned to benefit from the 9–11 tragedy. Immediately after 9–11, they were flooded with new buyers, unwilling to suffer the suddenly heightened inconvenience and time loss of ordinary commercial air travel. (One man's tragedy is always another's opportunity.)

The unused market space is not always in the middle, but there is often space between extremes of price or location. Sometimes, the space is at the top. At Glazer-Kennedy Insider's Circle™, we have a number of top cosmetic dentists with "Taj Mahal" spa-style offices featuring a wide array of patient comforts, from paraffin hand waxes and massage to lattes and fresh-baked cookies. Their average case fee is 200% to 500% higher than nearby, competing dentists. We even have a Member, a family psychologist in private practice, specializing in work with autistic children, who competes with free services available from government agencies as well as a number of other doctors in her area—and charges four times their average fees, and has a waiting list. I feature many examples of businesses finding opportunity at the top of pricing and their owners' thinking and strategies in my book *No B.S. Marketing to the Affluent*.

Sometimes the space is at the bottom—although I generally dislike this place. Still, Wal-Mart is, of course, the ultimate example of the moment, of grabbing empty space, both at the bottom of the price ladder and, initially, in locations other chains ignored.

Sometimes, it's in a means of distribution. My friend, the late E. Joseph Cossman, a mail-order guru, made ten different million-dollar businesses out of products sold by their manufacturers through only one or two means of distribution. He secured exclusive rights to the ignored distribution channels. My friend Joe Sugarman took sunglasses to TV infomercials, then QVC. Omaha Steaks and Allen Brothers: steaks sold by mail-order, delivered by FedEx.

Cosmetics, skin care products, and acne treatment products have long been at a number of different price points, from discount to outrageous, via department-store cosmetic counters, free-standing stores, mall kiosks, catalogs, and direct sales and networking marketing organizations like Avon, Amway, Mary Kay. My long-time client, Guthy-Renker, has virtually dominated distribution through TV infomercials for a decade, with its

Victoria Principal, Susan Lucci, Cindy Crawford, and other celebrity lines, and the Pro-Activ acne treatment products developed at my urging.

Looking for "The Gap" ideal for you to fill is a very nuts-and-bolts piece of advice, possibly more appropriate for one of my marketing books than this book. But I include it here for a broader purpose; illustration of the kind of thinking that attracts wealth. The cliché is "think outside the box." But I suppose it is a cliché because it is so laden with truth. Even savvy, clever, aggressive entrepreneurs fall into "inside the box" thinking. It's easy and dangerous to do. To see our opportunities only in terms of incremental improvements of what we already do and the way we do it, essentially pushing at the sides of the box. I take pride in the fact that clients who come to me for consulting days or are in coaching groups or attend Glazer-Kennedy Insider's Circle™ events frequently say the same thing—"I came to Kennedy thinking I was in one business; I left in an entirely different, infinitely better and more valuable business."

Information about my Renegade Millionaire System is online at www.RenegadeMillionaire.com.

Information about opportunities for association with innovative business owners in Glazer-Kennedy Insider's Circle™ on a national and local level, can be found at www.DanKennedy.com.

The challenge is to see what is not there. As example, consider this statement by the CEO of Home Depot, made in an interview in 2005:

Experts say we are in a $400-billion market, because that's the market for our products TODAY. But I say we are in a $900-billion market. We're focusing on selling differently to professional contractors and that's a $300-billion market itself. The "we-do-it-for-you" market is another $200-billion market itself.

In 2003–2004, this company experienced a 26% increase in sales of home installation and do-it-for-them services to what they called the "free-spending, do-it-for-me-now consumer."

Of course, if you carefully analyze all this, there's trading of dollars from one category to another, so adding each on top of the other is delusional. There are assumptions worthy of question. Subsequently, the hitting-the-wall of free-wheeling spending on home improvements by tapping ever-rising equity in homes made a mess of Home Depot's entire business. This CEO, Bob Nardelli, has since moved from Home Depot to the failed turnaround at Chrysler, but was still well enough thought of to be given an important position at Cerebrus, the private equity fund that owned Chrysler and had installed him there. With all that noted, and room for vastly differing opinions on Mr. Nardelli, still, the main point is the vision. The ability to see what was not yet there, to see gaps and opportunities, empty or under-served market space.

In The New Economy, there are all manner of new gaps, new market space, new opportunities to see what is not yet there that you may get to first.

In the February 17, 2005, issue of *USA Today*, there was an article in the Science Section headlined "A WHOLE NEW WAY OF LOOKING AT THE WORLD."

Bill Glazer used it as fodder for a sales letter about my Renegade Millionaire Retreat, saying "More important to me than just the millions of dollars I've made going in the directions Dan has pointed me is that, quite literally, Dan has shown me a whole new way of looking at the world."

He went on to write: "There are hundreds and hundreds of people who were in 'small businesses' who are now super-entrepreneurs with multiple streams of income they never imagined, with clientele they never conceived, charging prices or fees they never thought possible, being sought out rather than having to chase business."

I have the newspaper clipping up on my bulletin board as my own reminder of the mandate to keep looking at the world, at my world, at my clients' worlds in a whole new way—*frequently*.

How can you keep your thoughts about your own opportunities flexible, agile, outside rather than inside the box? The most important key is exposure, to a lot of ideas, information, news, business success stories, people outside the box of your business and your industry. I wrote another book in the No B.S. series just for this reason: *No B.S. DIRECT Marketing for NON-Direct Marketing Businesses*. It takes you inside very diverse examples of businesses using direct marketing, that customarily do not. You can't just read your trade journals; you need to read others' trade journals. Read good, well researched, cutting edge newsletters (like mine!). You need a lot of ideas, examples, and information flowing to you from diverse sources. I encourage people to be in coaching groups and mastermind groups, ours or others, with forward-thinking, forward-looking, flexible, innovative, and successful entrepreneurs in varied fields, not just their own.

Most entrepreneurs seem to operate as if Amish, locked away in a closed society. It's very, very hard to attract wealth working in a vacuum.

"But My Product IS Ordinary. It IS A Commodity."

Want my advice about that? If your product is ordinary, is a commodity, I suggest you just go off into the woods, deep into the woods, find an isolated place, sit, and meditate until life gently slips away and you are liberated from the torture of your banal existence by eternal rest. Or eaten by a bear.

I stopped adding to it years ago—the list of excuses/reasons why people can't use "my kind of" marketing, why they can't find anything interesting to say about their products or businesses, why they can't come up with a USP, why their business is, in fact, a commodity business and thus they must sell by price, etc. Before I stopped, the list was up over 100 excuses for being boring and failing to capture customers' imaginations. Well, I wonder if anything might be more of an ordinary commodity than a man's shirt. Most men don't like to shop and aren't that particular—a shirt's a shirt. Reading the new biography of Ogilvy sent me digging through all my Ogilvy files, which led me to Twitchell's book *20 Ads That Shook The World* and in turn to the ad by Ogilvy from 1951, one of an entire series of ads featuring his fictitious character The Baron (actor/model George Wrangell), the iconic man with the eye patch, wearing the Hathaway shirt. Just as the real Bond would never drink a martini stirred, not shaken, the Baron wouldn't be caught dead in any but a Hathaway shirt. Of course, a shirt is a shirt, but, to quote Twitchell, **when you cannot change what the product is, you have to change what it means.**

In this case, this shirt, the only shirt acceptable to the man in the eye patch, The Baron, was made to mean intrigue and sophistication. At the time—and I suppose still—women bought most of the men's dress shirts, so Ogilvy's man had to appeal to women, while also appealing differently to the 50+ executive wearing plain dress shirts for business. Ogilvy found George Wrangell, an occasional actor, and a real baron, a Russian, married into money. Ogilvy admits the eyepatch idea may have been suggested by the Hathaway company's CEO's wife, but rejected as too subtle and odd. Then on the way to the photo studio, he ducked into a drug store and bought one for $1.50, took it to the photo shoot, tried it, and decided to run with it after all. Stuck with a stone that could not be romanced—the basic white dress shirt, a staple of its time—Ogilvy focused instead on the man wearing the shirt as aspirational symbol.

These ads ran—incredibly—from 1951 to 1990 (39 years!!!) invigorating the moribund, lackluster Hathaway brand and making the company millions of dollars. Subsequent ads developed the Baron's character just as much but with mystery intact, and showed him in incredible scenes—conducting the New York Philharmonic at Carnegie Hall, fencing, sail-boating, and even—humorously—driving a tractor (a nod to Ogilvy's stint as a farmer), all the while wearing the perfectly pressed dress shirt.

If Ogilvy had followed the typical ad style of the '50s, the full-page ads would have shown the shirt—or his man in the shirt—with barely a line or two of copy beneath. But Ogilvy devoutly believed in (relatively) long copy no matter the product, thus brilliant copy like this:

> *American men are beginning to realize it is ridiculous to buy good suits and then spoil the effect by wearing an ordinary, mass-produced shirt. Hence the growing popularity of Hathaway shirts which are in a class by themselves.*

Of course, American men weren't "beginning to realize" anything of the sort until the ad suggested it. But that laid the foundation for the important rationale for this product—not spoiling the effect of the business suit. Oh, and who the devil says "hence," even in 1950? Nobody. But throughout this copy, antiquated language was used to deliberately sound "high-brow," to match the mysterious, obviously sophisticated fellow with the eye patch. In the descriptive copy about the shirt that follows, he even claims the shirt's stitching has "an antebellum elegance about it." What does that mean? Who knows? Who knew? The pitch concludes with:

> You get a great deal of quiet satisfaction out of wearing shirts which are in such impeccable taste.

The entire ad has over 230 words of copy, for a dress shirt sold at the department store.

Now, today, circa 2009, what Ogilvy did for this shirt is more important than ever. Consumers have more choices in every category. Recession-Think has made them much more reluctant to waste their money on anything ordinary, mundane, or unnecessary. The internet has served as a commoditizing force affecting almost every product and service category. If you insist on presenting your business, products, and services as incrementally better options within a range of ordinary and insist on selling with features and benefits (rather than transcending them), you will struggle mightily in The New Economy. My adaptation of Ogilvy's principles behind advertising like that done for Hathaway is that your business must be about something (other than selling things), about something profoundly meaningful to its clientele. In these times, that needs sharpening all the more. And just who the heck says "all the more"? No one. But me. I tried wearing an eye patch, too, but I kept bumping into things and missing my mouth with my spoon.

Wealth Magnet 18
No Boundaries

If you are my age, 50+, or even 40+, maybe even 30+, you are very likely to think provincially. You will have a preference for doing business with vendors within easy driving distance. If you own a local business, you will think mostly about local marketing to local customers. If you are under the age of 35, you will have grown up with the internet and that alone will have given you a very different viewpoint. Because I gravitated to what was then called "mail-order," and I never had a brick-and-mortar-only business, I never thought locally. On the other hand, though, because of my age, it's still more natural for me to think provincially than globally.

There are no geographic boundaries for wealth attraction. And most businesses can and should be enlarged and expanded to national or international scope. This is easy to understand in businesses like mine; information businesses. We can deliver a newsletter anywhere. The internet has accelerated and eased the global spreading of my persona and messages. While we always had a small number of subscribers and members overseas, today revenues from outside the United States are approaching 30% of our business. But *everybody* should get beyond local or regional to national or international. Let me give you a few examples.

Darin Garman was a real estate broker specializing in apartment buildings and commercial properties in Iowa. Naturally, most of his buyers and investors were also in Iowa. He was enormously successful, so he controlled more than 70% of all such transactions in his primary geographic market, Cedar Rapids and neighboring communities. At my urging, he began advertising nationally in publications like *Forbes* and *Investors Business Daily*, to interest investors all over America in the conservative "heartland of America" real estate investments. Today, more than half of all his sales of Iowa properties are to investors in New York, California, almost every other state, mostly sight unseen: he never even meets the investors in person. There are many benefits of bringing these investors in from all over America rather than just seeking them locally. For example, they are less price sensitive, not biased by what they "know" as are area residents; they are making their decisions purely based on the mathematical merits of the investment. Also, while there is obviously a limited, finite number of wealthy individuals interested in owning apartment buildings in Cedar Rapids, there's a virtually unlimited, infinite number of such wealthy individuals spread all over America.

Matt Furey, like me, is an author. His first book on fitness, still a bestseller (although never on a "bestseller list") is *Combat Conditioning*. For a long time, the only means for an author to attempt converting his knowledge and intellectual property to wealth was through bookstores, a very limited means of distribution, provincial multiplied. Matt chose to ignore the traditional publishing industry entirely, and has sold hundreds of thousands of copies entirely via his own direct-response ads in magazines and his web sites. But for Matt, the book is just the beginning. If you visit mattfurey.com, you'll enter a complex web of websites, e-mail newsletters, and other online marketing generating millions of dollars a year. Matt spends two months a year on combination vacation and research trips in China, spends an enormous amount of time with his family, works as he wishes. I've consulted with and coached Matt in the early stages of his business, and most recently sold one of my publishing companies to him (The Psycho-Cybernetics Foundation, www.psycho-cybernetics.com). His mastery of the internet makes a person in an isolated town in Afghanistan, a U.S. soldier on a base in a foreign land, a young man "with sand kicked in his face" in Africa just as viable a customer as someone working out at a local gym. But Matt is not alone, nor is the globally expansive power of the internet limited to books, tapes, and other information products.

Think of entire industries liberated from local or locale-to-locale boundaries by direct marketing; mail-order, toll-free numbers, the internet. It wasn't all that long ago that the only way you could buy or sell stocks was through your local broker at his local office. Antiques were sold in antique shops, art in galleries, not through eBay or on websites. We could fill the remainder of the book with examples.

Even the reach of the professional practice has gone from a five-mile radius to the world. You only need skim the pages of any airline's magazine, stuffed in the seat pockets, and you'll find full-page advertisements from cosmetic dentists, doctors treating carpel tunnel syndrome, doctors treating menopause. They advertise nationally, they attract patients who fly to them from all over the country. Why would someone who lives in Illinois go to a dentist in Houston, Texas? If you read this entire book carefully, you will understand the market forces and Wealth Attraction Magnets that make this happen. Incidentally, I live in Ohio, but my dentist is in Richmond, Virginia, and my financial advisor is in Durango, Colorado. I travel to the former several times a year. I never need to see the latter; all our business is easily done at distance. But in both cases, the controlling factor is expertise, not location.

When you transcend geographic boundaries, you instantly and automatically increase your wealth attraction power and opportunities.

This is a major issue for The New Economy. If you remain bound by geographic limitations, you will find yourself at ever-increasing disadvantage. Money is no longer concentrated anywhere, because people can do business from anywhere. During the month I was finishing this book, I flew to New York for a meeting with a very wealthy entrepreneur who has adopted the practice of taking his family to a different city each summer and living there for three months—this year New York, next year Paris. As he put it, "All I need is internet access. I can do business anywhere I choose to live." The idea of Wall Street as the capitol of finance, Manhattan as capitol of advertising, Dallas and Houston as twin capitols of oil, is antiquated. Money is more mobile and moving than ever before, so you must be too. The fastest practical way to attract more money is to broaden the territory from which you invite it.

The other important thing to remember about boundaries and The New Economy customer is that this customer expects easy and instant access. Think about the demise of the corner video store and the struggle for survival the biggest chain of such stores, Blockbuster, finds itself in, in the era of Netflix and instant movies on demand from your cable or satellite provider. A similar tempest is brewing with this thing you hold in your hands: books. The Kindle® and competing technology products give readers instant access to tens of thousands of books. You can instantly make books materialize on your iPhone®. The New Economy customer at his Caribbean island hideaway, where he can run his business by remote control, who hears of a book he is interested in on a morning financial news show need not try to find a bookstore or wait for delivery from Amazon; he can get it zapped to him instantly. Setting aside a long discussion about the destruction of intellectual property protections, the authors' interests, and the many reasons for developing your own library of treasured books in physical form, this still tentative evolution speaks to the "demand for now" that seems to increasingly control the movement of money, thus the attraction of wealth. Removal of physical boundaries and distances and related delays is the engineering feat of The New Economy.

Wealth Magnet 19
Clarity

I t's instructive to ask business owners how much money they expect to receive today, tomorrow, next week.

Most are playing blind archery. Few have clear, definite expectations. This is grievous negligence, as expectations have a great deal to do with results. It's also dereliction of managerial duty. It is up to you to decide—key word: *decide*—how much money you will receive today, this week, this month, this year, in advance, based upon your marketing and management plans, your pre-scheduled actions and initiatives. If you board an airplane and ask the pilot "Where are we going today? When are we scheduled to get there?" and he's not sure, exit immediately! For the pilot of a business, today's destination and arrival time is measured in dollars going into the bank account, customers captured for development, and a few other key pieces of data. If you're not sure about those things, the odds of arriving at the right destination by happy accident aren't good.

Ask a restaurant owner: "How much business are you going to do today?" He'll answer: "I don't know. It depends on who comes in." That's a lousy answer.

If you're running a restaurant, you have to have a very good idea of how many are coming in, if not who's coming in. You have a number of customers who've bought membership cards so you're dinging their credit cards the first of each month and sending them five coupons, you've sent a certain number of birthday cards out with coupons the week before, you've FAXed the week's specials to your business lunch customers, and you have certain expectations based on all this activity.

This gets us to the big topic of clarity. Clarity about what you don't want, what you do want, the income you expect, the net worth increases you expect, and the reasons for your expectations. I have long operated my businesses by numbers, knowing what the minimum amount my time must be worth, what a project must produce, what sales will come from an appearance in front of an audience. Tracking day by day, whether or not I am "on schedule" to hit my income *and* wealth targets for the week, month, quarter, year. If you don't know whether or not you are on schedule, it's a safe bet you aren't. If you're assessing how well you're doing with your goals for the year in October, it's too late. You need to assess how well you are doing at noon on January 2nd. And January 3rd, 4th, 5th.

I have clear, vivid mental pictures of what my business, business life, and personal life are to look like. I have detailed, constantly updated plans to support the pictures. I'm very clear about intentions and expectations. Sure, there's the axiom: if you want to hear God laugh, tell him your plans, and sure, things go awry. Fortunately, unexpected, better opportunities sometimes present themselves. But imperfect results from clarity are still far superior to random results. Clarity sets up magnetized targets you are drawn to. It allows your conscious and subconscious minds to work in tandem.

I'm also very clear about my schedule and work days. They aren't just planned, they are scripted, and well over 80% unfold exactly as scripted, producing exactly the results intended and expected. If this interests you, read the book *No B.S. Time Management for Entrepreneurs.*

Wealth is attracted to clarity. Paul J. Meyer, founder of Success Motivation Institute, a former insurance salesman who turned himself into a very wealthy entrepreneur with a number of business interests and extensive real estate investments, as well as an author on success subjects, said "If you are not achieving your goals, it is probably because they are not clearly defined." It's not that the individual lacks essential skills, opportunities, or resources to achieve his goals, or the ability to procure them, it is a problem with the goals themselves.

I have found, personally, the times that I wander astray from productivity and profit, and am not seeing the money stream in as it usually does for me, I've gotten foggy about my own intentions and objectives or negligent about measurement of progress.

Numbers

Chapter 43 in my book, *NO B.S. RUTHLESS MANAGEMENT OF PEOPLE AND PROFITS*, titled "Management by the Numbers (The Right Numbers)" describes in detail 13 different numerical and statistical measurements you should be tracking in your business constantly; some day to day, some week to week. These are not the numbers your accountant gives to you after the fact in historical documents, like financial statements and tax returns—these are living numbers you use to manage your business for maximum profit.

One of the attractants of wealth is respect for it, and one of the ways you can show that respect is by paying attention to and knowing the vital statistics in the source of your wealth, your business or businesses. You may recall the line from Kenny Rogers' song about never counting your money while sitting at the table 'cuz there's time enough for counting when the dealing's done. That was advice for *gamblers*, and it's based entirely on superstition. And the gambler dispensing the advice was dead broke. The most successful, wealthiest entrepreneurs I know and have known are on top of the important numbers.

In The New Economy there is less margin for error than ever. This does not mean you become the beady-eyed, tight-fisted bean counter worrying over the cost of paper clips, nor does it mean being a cheapskate always looking only for the cheapest bargain—which is, often, a false bargain. Entrepreneurs make poor accountants, and I'm not suggesting becoming one. And excessive anxiety about money attracts the polar opposite of wealth. On the other hand, you can't manage what you can't measure. Knowing THE RIGHT NUMBERS and using them in live-time decision-making (not historical analysis) is both pragmatic and motivational.

(*Available at all booksellers. Information online at www.NoBSBooks.com)

"I can zero in on a vision of where I want to be in the future. I can see it so clearly in front of me, when I daydream, it's almost a reality. Then I get this easy feeling, and I don't have to be uptight to get there because I already feel like I'm there, that it's just a matter of time.

"I set a goal, visualized it very clearly, then created the drive, the hunger for turning it into a reality. There's a kind of joy in that kind of ambition, in having a vision in front of you. With that kind of joy, discipline isn't difficult or negative or grim. You love doing what you have to do—going to the gym, working hard on the set. Even when pain is part of reaching your goal, and it usually is, you can accept that too."

—Arnold Schwarzenegger

Wealth Magnet 20
Independence

Wealth is attracted to wealth, money to money. But because independence is the prime outcome and benefit of wealth, wealth is also attracted to independence. One is as good as the other as a magnet.

Consequently, **the less you need income, the more opportunities present themselves, the more eager people are to do business with you and pay you money, the more easily wealth is attracted**. This mandates the simple practice of living beneath your present income, so that you can get and stay debt free.

There are major differences of opinion about this, but this is my book, so I will give you my opinion, based on what has worked so very well for me. I have been very consistent in my position on this, going back well before the most recent recession. I realize this is very conservative financial advice. But from my perspective, it is not just financial advice. It is directed at your inner being, subconscious mind, confidence, and outer behavior. It is, again, about attracting wealth more than it is part of a debate about using debt as investment capital. That debate ignores the psychology of attracting wealth.

Dave Ramsey, a popular radio and TV talk show host and personal finance expert I like and respect, who deals with money topics, agrees with me about getting and staying debt free for practical purposes. Many other financial gurus differ passionately. They might advise, for example, fully mortgaging your home in periods of low interest rate and investing that money in real estate or stocks or whatever, to make the spread, and build up assets. This was very popular advice in the years immediately preceding the recent bubbles bursting and stock market and housing market collapse. Many of the people who were most passionate about such advice—and most likely to ridicule "money chickens" like me—are now broke. I have never gotten comfortable with debt as an asset, with leveraging debt into more debt. I also have a much longer view of history than most seem to have. I remember, for example, the Jimmy Carter years and the Houston real estate crash, when people so leveraged were wiped out en masse. I also find that the leverage-the-debt advice often comes from people who earn commissions selling investments. However, here, now, this is not about that debate. The debate ignores and omits the psychology of attracting wealth by feeling, at your core, wealthy (not indebted), and by feeling and being independent.

Debt doesn't just enslave through compound interest reversed. It enslaves by imposition, by telling you that you should do work you don't want to do, accept clients or customers you can't stand, and otherwise compromise every which way because you need money. I insist your objective should be to get to the position of not needing more income, so you can act independent, be selective, call your own shots, entirely free of actual or felt pressure. What I call "The Independent Position" rolls

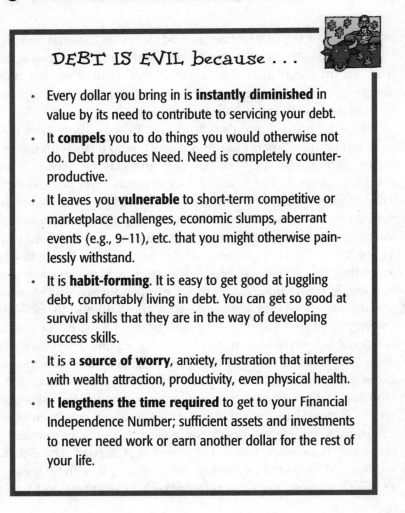

DEBT IS EVIL because . . .

- Every dollar you bring in is **instantly diminished** in value by its need to contribute to servicing your debt.

- It **compels** you to do things you would otherwise not do. Debt produces Need. Need is completely counter-productive.

- It leaves you **vulnerable** to short-term competitive or marketplace challenges, economic slumps, aberrant events (e.g., 9–11), etc. that you might otherwise pain-lessly withstand.

- It is **habit-forming**. It is easy to get good at juggling debt, comfortably living in debt. You can get so good at survival skills that they are in the way of developing success skills.

- It is a **source of worry**, anxiety, frustration that interferes with wealth attraction, productivity, even physical health.

- It **lengthens the time required** to get to your Financial Independence Number; sufficient assets and investments to never need work or earn another dollar for the rest of your life.

finances, attitude, reality and emotions, conscious and subconscious together, and it is magic.

Everybody needs to be cautious of *need*. After all, if you ask most people why they go to work in the morning, they say: to pay bills. Very high income people say the same thing. And they are still slaves, just better dressed. Working for Debt.

Entrepreneurs need to be especially cautious of expanding *need* by piling on employees, infrastructure, overhead, people, places, and things. Bigger is not necessarily better. More gross may not only produce less net, but may move you from master to slave before you realize it. I once, briefly, worked as a business owner to meet the payroll, pay the bills, re-stock the inventory, getting any scraps that might be left over. I didn't like it. And it put me into a mental state completely antithetical to wealth attraction.

In my *Renegade Millionaire System* (www.renegademillionaire .com), I devote a large amount of time and energy to defining and extolling the virtues of "autonomy." I believe it is THE objective that should govern the setting of all other objectives, and that it is a closed loop: the pursuit of autonomy best attracts wealth, which facilitates autonomy.

Whether through debt-reduced or debt-free living, other strategies—like improving deal flow, psychological techniques, or all of these things—I can assure you, the less you *need* the next deal, the next sale, the next client, the next dollar, the easier it will be to attract all the deals, sales, clients, and dollars you could ever desire or imagine, times ten.

Wealth Magnet 21
Think Value, Not Time

People in prison "do time." Unless you are reading this book while actually behind bars, you don't want to indulge in this same kind of thinking.

People in prison, i.e., criminals, are not the only people who try to steal money. Actually a lot of people who appear to be stand-up citizens go through their entire lives trying to steal money. Many succeed but only to a limited degree. Their theft stands in the way of attracting wealth and abundance. Their theft puts them in a prison of their own making.

People who work in factories, especially if union employees, think years on the job should translate to wage increases. This is why wage-earners rarely attract wealth. Their erroneous, greedy thinking is in the way. Although it is corporate CEOs and entrepreneurs usually accused by the media and viewed by the public

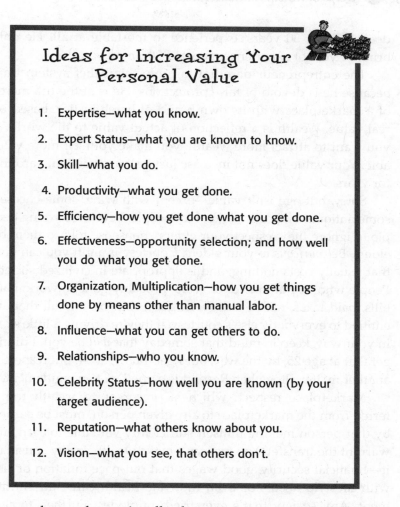

Ideas for Increasing Your Personal Value

1. Expertise—what you know.

2. Expert Status—what you are known to know.

3. Skill—what you do.

4. Productivity—what you get done.

5. Efficiency—how you get done what you get done.

6. Effectiveness—opportunity selection; and how well you do what you get done.

7. Organization, Multiplication—how you get things done by means other than manual labor.

8. Influence—what you can get others to do.

9. Relationships—who you know.

10. Celebrity Status—how well you are known (by your target audience).

11. Reputation—what others know about you.

12. Vision—what you see, that others don't.

as greedy—and occasionally there are some spectacularly conscienceless thieves who work their way to top spots on Wall Street (as we've recently seen) or at big corporations—it is actually these rank-and-file wage workers who exhibit greed at its worst. They want something for nothing, they seek an unfair exchange. Time on a job, years doing a job, does not increase the inherent value of that job being done. In most cases, after the first few years, it doesn't increase the value of the employee either. He doesn't bring 30 years' experience to the table at all. He only brings 1 year of experience repeated 30 times.

The entrepreneur dare not fall into this belief system trap, because he is devoid of false protections. He is at the full mercy of a marketplace with its own brand of harsh justice, based on real value. Wealth is a reflection of actual value to the world. If you want to attract more wealth, you make yourself more valuable. Your value does not increase just because you hang around for years.

Sorry, but age isn't value—except with wine, some cheeses, some antiques and collectibles. Not people. I even tell young people to ignore the "respect your elders" nonsense told to them by elders. Be *courteous* to your elders. Courtesy is a gift you can give that usually costs nothing, and is appropriate in civilized society. People who've put in a lot of years, probably gone to work, paid bills, paid taxes, raised kids, been good citizens, and all that are entitled to everybody else's courtesy. If they're driving a little slow in your way, keep in mind that someday that *will* be you. I didn't get that at age 25, by the way, but I get it now, at 54. But respect is another matter altogether. Respect is earned, not an entitlement.

Marketplace respect, which is precursor to wealth transferred from the marketplace to any given person, must be earned by that person making himself sufficiently valuable to earn and warrant the transfer. You just can't make wealth or any cousin of it—financial security, good wages that out-pace inflation or rise with lifestyle needs, or even first rate health care—an entitlement. Any society that's ever tried, implodes. Further, foolish attempts to do so deliver a false and harmful message to people. Regardless of their folly, though, the truth can set you free: You can only be assured of getting whatever you want out of life, whether a certain income or security or wealth or simple respect, by earning it through proportionate creation of value. Not just getting older and being here or there longer.

One of my Members, Judith Z. told me of one of her employees, who every year comes to her and needs a raise. Because they need it you are, of course, obligated to give it. That's how they think. I've hung around for another year, so I'm entitled to more money. I need more money so I should get it. This is how they think. You can never think this way. Owning your business for ten years does not entitle you to anything more than your newest competitor of one year. What you get comes from the value you create and deliver.

Let me illustrate how completely devoid of integrity this time-on-the-job thinking is. You own a convenience store and you sell coffee for $1.00 per cup. Every morning, the same customer comes in, gets a cup of coffee, pays his dollar. After a year, he comes in and points a gun at your head. He says "I've been here everyday for a year. That's tenure. I've been exchanging a dollar for a cup of coffee. Solely because I've made that value exchange for a year, I'm now going to take two cups of coffee for the same one dollar and you're going to let me or I'll shoot you in the head."

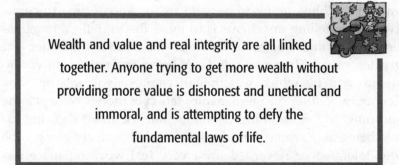

> Wealth and value and real integrity are all linked together. Anyone trying to get more wealth without providing more value is dishonest and unethical and immoral, and is attempting to defy the fundamental laws of life.

So the employee comes to Judith Z. every year and needs her annual raise. And every year, Judith sits down with her and says, "Fine, you've got a raise, as soon as you enroll in this course and you go to this seminar and you study these books and recordings. And as soon as you do, your raise is a done deal. Not after you finish. As soon as you do these three things and get started, the raise is a done deal."

My question to her was, "How many years have you gone without giving her a raise?"

Her answer is, "14."

This employee wants more money but is unwilling to do anything to deliver more value.

You must avoid making the same unreasonable demands, the same demands devoid of integrity, of the universe. Instead, if you'd like to attract more wealth, do the opposite. Do something that increases the value you bring to your business, your work, your clients or customers. Increase your value and you will attract increased wealth.

Recently, we've had a gigantic, very unpleasant and uncomfortable economic enema, and one of the things flushed out was a big, big, big turd comprised of far too many people trying to get paid far too much for providing too little value. They got flushed out of executive suites at the top of tall buildings, flushed off factory floors, flushed out of small businesses. The New Economy will not welcome them back. A new level of harsh reality about value is, I think, going to be with us for a long time to come. What I am telling my clients is to focus their intellect, imagination, and initiative as never before on the creation of greater and greater value. This may wind up being the only pathway to wealth and by which wealth will come to you in The New Economy. Neither the mere manipulation of money or paper, the shuffling and re-shuffling of things, nor the mere showing up and being at the same place for an extended term are going to be well-tolerated or rewarded. In a very real way, the space has shrunk, there's less room at the inn, and those who bring little may not get in.

Wealth Magnet 22
Think Equity, Not Income

This is big.

Most entrepreneurs wake up every morning thinking about how they can make more sales, get more customers, increase their incomes. These thoughts are ricocheting around their heads even as they stumble toward the bathroom or coffeemaker. And most entrepreneurs devote enormous thought, time, energy to these same issues all day long, all month long, all year long. At the end of each day, they try to assess how their day turned out in terms of income. But very few entrepreneurs give the same thought, time and energy to increasing "value" and "equity."

Income is temporary and perishable. Value and equity can be built to last. Right now, your daily thoughts, your daily measurements are probably weighted 80%, 90%, even 100% to increasing income, only 20%, 10%, or 0% to increasing value and equity. The right balance is 50%/50%.

How can you possibly manage and measure increases in equity daily, like you can income? Actually, there are a number of ways. One of the best is what I call Future Banking.

Most business owners are focused on Present Banking. If you ask a restaurant operator how his day was, he might cite number of meals served, number of customers who came in, or sales. But he will not talk about any measured equity increase. That's what I call Future Banking, and he will not have given it a thought.

I teach Future Banking in a lot of depth in my *Wealth Attraction System* and *Renegade Millionaire System**. Here, a simplified summary. First, income is income and does not necessarily convert to wealth. In fact, income is usually spent. Income increases do not necessarily translate to wealth either. Wealth is wealth. It comes from "value" and "equity." Second, there is Present Banking and Future Banking. The really astute entrepreneur works on both simultaneously, not sequentially. He thinks about "value," not just "income."

Information about my Renegade Millionaire System is online at www.RenegadeMillionaire.com.

Information about opportunities for association with innovative business owners in Glazer-Kennedy Insider's Circle™ on a national and local level, can be found at www.DanKennedy.com.

We'll use our restaurant owner again as example. My client, Dean Killingbeck of Get Customers Now, has developed a phenomenally successful direct-mail marketing campaign used by thousands of restaurants, using the birthdays of every customer, and even creating lists in any geographic area of people having birthdays month by month. They are mailed actual birthday cards that contain special offers good the week of their birthday or weeks surrounding it. This works because nobody celebrates a birthday alone, and the number-one way birthdays are celebrated is going out to a restaurant. Each birthday brings 2 to 8 people in the door. This is very reliable. Name the type of restaurant and he can tell you what each birthday on file is worth in dollars, year after year. So let's say a birthday captured is worth $100.00 a year to Restaurant Owner Bob. Now at the end of the night, Bob has a deposit for his Present Bank Account *and* another deposit for his Future Bank Account. For his Present Bank Account, the night's revenues of $20.00 times 200 diners, $4,000.00 less costs, $2,000.00. But his wait staff also got names, e-mail addresses, addresses, and birthdays from 37 first time customers. Bob deposits $3,700.00 in his Future Bank Account.

It is this "operating principle" that built up the wealth in my business over a 15-year period. For example, every time I got on an airplane and schlepped somewhere to speak, I made $10,000.00 or $20,000.00 or $30,000.00 to as much as $50,000.00 from the fee plus the books and courses sold, less my costs of goods, travel, overhead, to deposit in my Present Bank Account. But in my business, each newly acquired customer was known to be worth thousands of dollars in Future Bank value. So every day, my Future Bank deposit was much, much larger than my Present Bank deposit. So it stacked up year after year, pushing more and more additional income forward. As it peaked, I was able to extract millions from my businesses and also sell my businesses.

To the degree that the Future Bank value of whatever you do today matches or exceeds the Present Bank value, you set in motion wealth *creation* forces that will soon deliver a massive harvest. Further, when you see your Future Bank balance building exponentially, your sense of being wealthy grows, and that sense or (mental) state of being wealthy *attracts* more wealth. A big, accurately, and legitimately calculated Future Bank balance has all the same positive effects as does or would an equally large Present Bank balance. You think differently, feel differently, speak differently, act differently, and are perceived more favorably by others when you are wealthy, secure, and independent than when you are not. Your Future Bank balance can give this to you faster.

From a psychological standpoint, it's extremely beneficial to have a Future Bank System working for you in your business. From a practical standpoint, in The New Economy, it is more essential than ever, because the costs of creating present income have risen and are rising, and the tax bite taken out of higher earners' present incomes is more substantial and likely to worsen in response to the massive deficits and expansion of government in general and entitlement programs specifically occurring under the Obama administration. All this makes each dollar of Present Income worth less, and makes it much more difficult to build wealth by moving dollars from present, day-to-day income to savings and investments. You need financial leverage, not just income, and leverage is most likely to be found in Future Banking, not Present Banking.

Wealth Magnet 23
Marketing Prowess

H ere is THE secret of secrets about the entrepreneurs who create and attract great wealth with relative ease, and are sought after by other wealthy entrepreneurs, executives, and investors who are eager to do business with them.

These super-entrepreneurs may not be able to find their car keys, keep their offices free of overwhelming clutter, read a balance sheet, or turn on a computer. What they *don't* know would shock most people. Their personality flaws and personal dysfunctions could keep teams of psychotherapists gainfully employed. But one thing is true of virtually every single one of them:

They are unabashed, unashamed, irrepressible promoters, salespeople who know how to sell and do so day in and day out, and understand and usually keep their hands on their firms' marketing. They are, first and foremost, marketers.

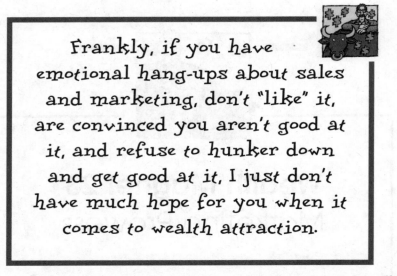

Frankly, if you have emotional hang-ups about sales and marketing, don't "like" it, are convinced you aren't good at it, and refuse to hunker down and get good at it, I just don't have much hope for you when it comes to wealth attraction.

Some entrepreneurs good at other things try delegating all the marketing. I've yet to see that go well. I see them delegate just about everything else with liveable results. But not the marketing. And really, why should you be able to delegate the money-getting and still wind up getting the money?

I'll tell you an instructive story. For about a year, I had a major corporation, owned by a big global conglomerate, as a client. You'd know the names. The CEO was a pleasant fellow good at holding meetings, counting the beans, managing. But he was totally clueless about how to get customers. The company's several hundred franchisees wanted to lynch him. His ad agency was scamming him. I was busily straightening his mess out, replacing embarrassingly inane and ineffective advertising with something persuasive and powerful. One day, he sat down with me in his office, door firmly closed, and told me he'd run some numbers and was distressed to discover I was being paid a big multiple of what he was being paid, on an hourly basis—"and, after all," he said, "I am the CEO here."

I said, "That's OK. There's a very good reason why you're paying me so much more per hour than you can pay yourself.

You know how to do everything here far better than I do, maybe better than anybody else, except for one little thing. I know how to get customers for you. You don't. But without what I know everything you know is worthless. But, don't let this worry you. We'll keep this our little secret."

Here's the undeniable fact about my wealth: People have been attracted to me, line up and literally wait and beg and compete for my attention, and stay glued to me if they can for one reason and one reason only. It's not my warm 'n' fuzzy personality. It's because I know how to get customers for them. I see opportunities in their businesses they are blind to. So they tolerate my quirks and unusual demands and business practices. They pay very high fees, and stay even when I raise fees with impunity. If you know marketing, you are in the ultimate power position.

Arnold Schwarzenegger got a part he wanted, at the strident objections of the director, because the studio heads knew no other star who knew how to promote a movie like Arnold. They told the director, if it's you or him, it's you. That's how it works in the real world. The least dispensable person with the most power is the person who can bring in money. *The Apprentice* became an astounding TV success and, behind the scenes, an enormous financial success for NBC, Mark Burnett, and Trump not just because it was a great show—it was—but more because

---

POWER UP YOUR MARKETING PROWESS

with my books *No B.S. DIRECT Marketing for NON-Direct Marketing Businesses* and *No B.S. Sales Success*, from bookstores or online booksellers. Get my *No B.S. Marketing Letter* as part of the free gift offer on page 250.

Donald Trump is an incredible, relentless promoter. I recently had a client, who must remain nameless, sell his company for an outrageous 15-times multiple of earnings because the bigger competitor was simply worn out and frustrated with competing with his superior marketing. They paid just to make him stop.

Every entrepreneur I know who has "money magnetism" also has exceptional marketing prowess.

Wealth Magnet 24
Behavioral Congruency

Behavioral Congruency is *the core idea behind my* entire *Renegade Millionaire System*.

It is a deceptively simple idea, contrary to the overwhelming majority of all self-improvement and success literature. It doesn't negate anything in any of the thousands of other how-to-succeed or how-to-get-rich books, courses, or seminars, but I do say it is more important than anything in those books.

Most approaches to becoming more successful or prosperous focus on attitudes and thoughts. But, as a result of 30 years' work with hundreds of first generation, from-scratch millionaire and multi-millionaire entrepreneurs, and my current work with so many million-dollar-a-year earners and wealthy entrepreneurs I came to one major conclusion:

It's less about how they *think* than about what they *do*.

Just for example, I worked 12 hours today, on a Sunday, on this book. I didn't wake up highly motivated to do that. I wasn't inspired by a muse. Nor did I try to get inspired or motivated or find somebody to motivate me. I didn't need to listen to a motivational recording. I didn't waste even a minute trying to modify my attitude. **I just went to work** and wrote, because I had an imminent deadline and I prize keeping my commitments above just about everything else. That's what I do. I work to meet deadlines. This is all about behavior, not "positive thinking."

Sure, that's little more than self-imposed, situation-imposed discipline. But there's another layer that goes on top of this that's even more important. Step #1 is: Behavior. But advanced wealth attraction Step #2 is: Congruent Behavior.

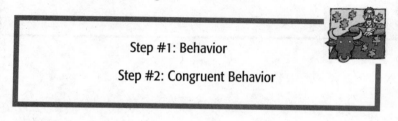

Step #1: Behavior

Step #2: Congruent Behavior

Congruent with *what*?

First—and this is key—**congruent with the behavior of people already achieving the goals you want to achieve,** already living the kind of life you want to live. This is called "modeling." Find them, study them, model them. And model their behavior. Don't worry too much about their thinking or attitudes. It's what they do and how they do it that matters most.

If your behavior is incongruent with the behavior of the people who enjoy the kinds of successes to which you aspire, you can't get those kinds of successes. Simple example: top golfers use great coaches and practice regularly and frequently. If you are too cheap to get a great coach or too lazy or busy to practice, you can forget about being a top golfer. And you can "be motivated" and "think positive" and "visualize" all you want, bubba, you still ain't going to be a top golfer!

> "By following your behavioral goals, you get to your objectives.
>
> "Instead of trying to break par, a result we cannot control, we concentrate on putting a good swing on the ball, an action we can control. The distinction is crystal clear, surely, but it never ceases to amaze me that the same folks in my workshops who nod their heads in agreement with the golf analogy turn right around and announce that their goal in this negotiation is to sign the deal and collect the money. So I ask you again: Is this signing and collecting something you can actually control? What you can control is behavior and activity, what you cannot control is the result of this behavior and activity.
>
> "Think behavior, forget result."
>
> —JIM CAMP, AMERICA'S #1 NEGOTIATING COACH,
> AUTHOR, *START WITH NO*, WWW.CAMPMETHOD.COM.

On the other hand, the quicker you align your present behavior with the behavior of people who already have, are achieving, and are experiencing the results to which you aspire, the faster you get those results. In fact, the result will so closely follow the behavior alignment it will seem instant.

Second, **congruent with the goals themselves**. Consider a goal to lose 40 pounds. Dropping by the doughnut shop every morning is incongruent behavior. Stocking your pantry with cookies, incongruent. Going out with friends to a place that only serves pizza, incongruent. Taking the elevator up to only the second floor instead of walking up the stairs, incongruent. The quicker you re-arrange your behaviors to be congruent with the goal, the quicker you get the goal. The more behaviors you adopt and adhere to that are congruent with the goal, the more certain you are to achieve it—automatically.

Most people are, bluntly, bullshitters—b.s.'ing themselves! What could be worse than lying to yourself? But if you claim a goal but behave in ways incongruent with the goal, you're a b.s.'er.

With regard to wealth, if you get your behavior congruent with whatever your wealth goals are, and congruent with the behavior of others who've achieved your wealth goals, it is an absolute certainty that your wealth will come flowing in—probably faster than you would have imagined. In fact, there is a thing I call The Phenomenon. Every wealthy entrepreneur I work with has experienced it at least once, most several times, in their lives. Personally, three times for me, including right now. The Phenomenon is when you accomplish more or attract more wealth in 12 months than in the previous 6 years, or some similarly amazing ratio. For most, The Phenomenon seems to just happen. Most think "finally!" But The Phenomenon can actually be made to happen, can be helped along and accelerated, because it is little more than a reflection of both kinds of Behavioral Congruency converging. You can't directly make The Phenomenon happen, but you can make Behavioral Congruency happen.

The more aligned you are
with the things you want,
the more powerfully
you attract them.

The things you
congruently want
have no choice
but to be
attracted to you.

People who are
congruent are
attractive,
magnetic—even
charismatic.

When you are fully congruent,
you are irresistible.

—MARK VICTOR HANSEN, CO-AUTHOR OF *CHICKEN SOUP FOR THE SOUL* AND ROBERT ALLEN, AUTHOR OF *NOTHING DOWN AND CREATING WEALTH*. FROM THEIR BOOK, *THE ONE MINUTE MILLIONAIRE*, WWW.ONEMINUTEMILLIONAIRE, WWW.MARKVICTORHANSEN.COM.

Wealth Magnet 25
Act Wealthy to Attract Wealth

There are actually *two Wealth Magnets here that* work in concert as one. One half will seem obvious and logical, but the other will seem completely illogical, and will be very difficult to accept. It usually takes hours to present properly, and the equal of that in pages just isn't available here. So I can only caution you against using one Magnet without the other, and encourage you to try **The 90-Day Experiment** that I suggest here. *You need not have any confidence in it working for it to work. You only need to do it for 90 days.* You'll see results. You'll be amazed. Then you'll stick with it even though you may never be able to logically explain it to anyone else, just as I can't logically explain it to you.

First, let's get clear about what I'm NOT talking about here: "act as if." In a lot of "wealth seminars," the speakers encourage you to buy new clothes, new cars, a mansion, start living the lifestyle of the rich and famous, and essentially pretend to be rich, somehow fooling yourself and others. Their idea is "pretend and money will follow." Actually, most people experience "pretend and bankruptcy will follow." However, they are onto something when it comes to fooling your subconscious. If you act in ways that the wealthy really act, you set in motion a big collection of internal changes and external effects that do attract wealth. It so happens I know hundreds of very wealthy people intimately, almost all first-generation rich, entrepreneurs who've made it from scratch. A few are "new-money flashy"—private jets, big mansions, bling bling. Most are not. Most behave more like the millionaires described in detail by Thomas Stanley in his book *The Millionaire Next Door* and his other research. But there are two things all really wealthy people do, that you can mimic, and that will have surprisingly dramatic, positive, wealth-attracting effects.

The logical one is: saving. Systematic, disciplined saving. This is important because wealth is not about income. Most people focus only on increasing income. But the wealthy are just as concerned or more concerned with increasing equity. So, here's The 90-Day Experiment: immediately establish a new bank account and call it your Wealth Account. It can be checking, interest-bearing checking, money market. At first, it doesn't matter. Next, determine a fixed percentage of every dollar that comes your way that will be diverted into that Wealth Account. Something between 1% and 10%. You may think you can't do this—hey, I can't pay my bills now with 100% of every buck, how will I pay them with 90%? Well, maybe you won't. But you aren't now either! So just do it. Pick a percentage, deposit the money, and then do NOT touch it, no matter what. And make these deposits every time a dollar arrives. Daily if need be. The more often the better. The act of putting money into your Wealth Account does things to and through your subconscious mind that cannot be fully explained. The amount matters a lot less than the act. You could be poor, getting paid $10.00 a day, decide on 1%, and be putting only 10-cents a day into a piggy bank, and even though you would directly accumulate little in 90 days, so many other things would change in your life, you'd still be amazed.

If you feel like reading about the core practicality of this, try the classic book *Richest Man in Babylon* by George Clason.

Anyway, make a deposit to your Wealth Account of a pre-determined percentage of EVERY dollar you receive.

If you do take money out during The 90-Day Experiment, you MUST limit it to true investment. If, for example, you are paying a home mortgage or auto loan, and have enough in the Wealth Account to pay an extra monthly principal payment, that's acceptable. But NOT to pay your regular monthly payment. That's not kosher.

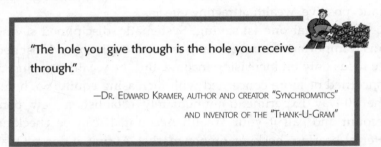

"The hole you give through is the hole you receive through."

—Dr. Edward Kramer, author and creator "Synchromatics" and inventor of the "Thank-U-Gram"

Now here comes the completely illogical one: giving. This is important because all wealthy people give. Giving has an incredible effect on your psyche. So, immediately open another separate bank account and call it your Giving Account. Also pre-determine a fixed percentage of every dollar that you receive to divert to your Giving Account. There, you will build up amounts to give to your charities, churches, people in need, even over-tip hard-working people. If you take money out during The 90-Day Experiment, which I encourage, it must be to give away with no direct quid pro quo or expectation of return or gain, and it should not replace giving you already do, such as whatever you now drop into the church collection plate every Sunday.

Obviously, it's hard to imagine how SUBTRACTING 10% from your income and giving it away can increase your income or wealth. 100% minus 10% = 90%. $10,000.00 minus $1,000.00 = $9,000.00. But, somehow, this math works more like this: 100% - 10% = 100% x 4 = 400%.

The first time I heard this from Foster Hibbard, I thought he was nutty as my grandmother's fruitcake. I don't blame you for thinking I'm smoking crack. But I assure you, try it for 90 Days, and you'll be a convert.

Later, by the way, you can get more sophisticated. Your Wealth Account money can move through the account into various investments. Personally, for my Giving Account, I use a charitable trust account with Fidelity Investments, that puts the money in my choice of Fidelity funds, dispenses donations as I direct, and provides the charitable tax deduction the year I deposit the funds whether they are dispensed that same year or not. Others create their own foundations. There are also complex issues, like donation of appreciated assets free of capital gains taxes. But all that can wait. First, run The 90-Day Experiment.

The Power of Habitforce

We *are* creatures of habit.

You probably do your morning regimen the same way every morning by habit. Drive to certain destinations the same way every time by habit. Maybe have exactly the same argument with spouse or friend again and again by habit. You either leave the toothpaste tube cap off or put it on by habit.

By adopting, installing, and controlling certain "habits of wealthy entrepreneurs," you put habitforce on your side, as a means of naturally attracting wealth. Napoleon Hill discovered such habits in common in the hundreds of exceptional entrepreneurs and achievers he researched and interviewed from 1917 to 1935, in preparation of the publication of his works, *Laws of Success* and *Think and Grow Rich*. In my more up-close, personal, intense, and involved work with hundreds of from-scratch millionaire and multi-millionaire entrepreneurs, I have also observed certain habits in common; hundreds of differences but a few habits held in common.

These two habits are almost universal in these wealthy entrepreneurs. No, most do not do them as mechanically and rigidly as I have described here, although quite a few did when they adopted the habits at my suggestion. I am more flexible with myself now, and tend to make Wealth deposits only a few times a month, Giving deposits the same, and I actually no longer have a single Wealth Account and, instead, track it all on paper in a mythical account summarizing all my investments. But in the beginning, I made my deposits religiously, frequently, every time money arrived, exactly as Foster described to me. If it's all new and foreign to you, I urge beginning within rigid rules.

Always Bear Left

Quite a few years ago, a friend of mine with very eclectic interests spent a lot of time studying how people behaved in all sorts of situations and circumstances. One of the things that came out of it was his book titled *Always Bear Left*, so named as advice on getting in the shortest lines the majority of the time. He found that the majority of people move to the right and get in lines furthest away from the line or lines furthest to their left, presumably because more people are right-handed than left-handed, so they habitually think right first. They are drawn to the lines to their right by habitforce.

Dr. Maxwell Maltz, author of the original *Psycho-Cybernetics*, and co-author with me of *The New Psycho-Cybernetics*, developed the concept of the Self-Image as a navigational device and governor of both behavior and achievement. Dr. Maltz explained that trying to act in conflict with your own self-image by means of conscious, deliberate, teeth-gritted, fists-clenched willpower can only be sustained in short bursts for short periods of time, then a snap-back effect occurs. This explains the dieter falling off the diet drastically with episodes of binge eating. Rather than fighting your own self-image with willpower, Dr. Maltz suggested re-programming the self-image so that behavior congruent with your objectives could occur naturally. He spoke of this as replacing an Automatic Failure Mechanism with an Automatic Success Mechanism.

If you combine these concepts, you can see just how much we are controlled by habitforce. What we have thought is what we think, what we have done is what we do. Changing your attractiveness to wealth and thus your actual wealth has to be preceded by changing your habits.

In this context, consider The New Economy. It is more demanding than its parent of those to whom it will give wealth. Old habits of thought and personal behavior and business practice must be replaced with new ones compatible with its new demands.

Ultimately, habitforce either works for you or against you.

Consider a simple thing such as getting to work. Most people have the habit of getting to their workplace and then wandering around, engaging in trivial conversation with others while getting coffee in the break-room or from the café across the street, looking at the newspaper, and finally shuffling papers before deciding what they are going to do first. I have developed the habit of organizing my first work of the day the night before, assigning start and stop times to my planned tasks, and going directly from my bed down the stairs to my office and immediately getting into my work. Who do you think has more accomplished by 9:00 A.M. each morning? I give myself advantage. Others handicap themselves. Way back when, when I was in outside sales, I formed the habit of setting up breakfast meetings at clients' businesses, arriving with coffee and pastry at 8:00 A.M.—which forced me to get to productive work early everyday. Other salespeople putter around and procrastinate most of most mornings. When you commit to highly productive habits, you build up an Automatic Success Mechanism. You put habitforce on your side as an ally.

Wealth Magnet 26
Energy From People

There are very practical obstacles to wealth attraction that short circuit your wealth attraction.

The first big obstacle is incompetent people. Sometimes these are people incapable of handling the responsibilities or doing the jobs entrusted to them. More frequently these are people able but unwilling to do the jobs. They are lazy and uncreative. They have no sense of urgency or initiative, so they will do only the minimum, they will not figure out solutions, they will let their progress be stalled by the slightest challenge, and return everything to your lap. Dealing with such people is a miserable, sadly common experience. Every entrepreneur wrestles with these people. They may be employees, vendors, advisors, others.

Another, related obstacle: people who waste or abuse your time, what I call "time vampires." This bunch can just as easily include certain clients or customers as employees and vendors.

Another, related obstacle: People who drain or divert your mental energy, who disrupt the flow of your wealth attraction. Negative people, gloom 'n' doom people, whiners and complainers. Mike Vance, former Dean of Disney University, calls them pissers and moaners. This bunch can just as easily include friends and relatives as employees, vendors, customers, or clients.

They must all go. The minute you detect their toxic odor, take action to get them out of your business, out of your life, to distance yourself from them. You need to develop a Zero Tolerance Policy about all these people and be decisive, even ruthless in enforcing it. Hesitancy and timidity in doing so will always cost you more than whatever temporary trauma and disruption results from making changes in your staff, vendors, or others around you. Always.

I'll give you a very common example. A client with five staff members in his office brought me in, to observe, interview, analyze, look at his business from top to bottom with my "fresh eyes." I told him that his majorette domo, his key office manager, the employee who had been with him the longest had to go. I told him she was sabotaging his new initiatives behind his back, ignoring procedures he wanted followed, damaging morale, and driving away good clients. I told him she was the equal of an open vat of toxic chemicals. He insisted he needed her, relied on her, couldn't function without her; at bare minimum, the disruption caused by firing her would be disastrous. It took me over a year to convince him to give the old battleax the ax. Immediately after doing so, sales increased; he made no other changes; no increased advertising; she exited, enter more income. Within the year, the business was 30% more profitable, the remaining employees measurably more productive, my client happier, more relaxed, and more productive. By the following year, his net worth had increased by nearly $500,000.00, and he had enough liberated time to finally launch a second business he'd been back-burnering for years. A "wealth block" had been surgically removed, vibrant health created by its removal.

Think of your wealth attraction power as electric current. Years ago, strings of Christmas lights could be short-circuited by any loose bulb, any burnt-out bulb or any bad fuse. If there was one of these anywhere in the entire string of lights, it disrupted the flow of power, and the entire string shut off. I remember helping my father unscrew and test bulb after bulb, fuse after fuse, to find the one bad one. The power cord that runs between you and the world supply of wealth and the world supply of wealth and you has a very similar flaw. One disruptive person laying a finger on it anywhere along the line shuts down the entire flow of power.

I try my level best to operate a Zero Tolerance Policy toward people who disrupt the flow of my wealth attraction power. Be they employee, vendor, associate, or client, I will not tolerate their interference with the flow of wealth to me. I rid myself of them, even if at considerable, temporary cost. I have, on several occasions, stopped projects for clients after I've done a lot of work on them, refunded as much as $70,000.00, just to get rid of the client who was a "problem child," seriously interfering with my flow of power.

One of my rules:

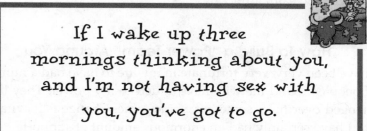

If I wake up three mornings thinking about you, and I'm not having sex with you, you've got to go.

Most people tolerate others causing them undue stress and aggravation, without realizing how costly such tolerance is. I want you to understand: it is very, very costly.

The opposite of all this is the assembly and organization of your own small cadre of exceptionally competent, highly creative, extraordinarily reliable and trustworthy individuals who are in sync and harmony with you and your objectives, who facilitate and even multiply your wealth attraction power. If you read Lee Iacocca's autobiography, you saw his description of this as his "horses," the few key people he relied on. If you carefully observed Donald Trump during his *Apprentice* television programs, read his books, and read his biography, you realized that George Ross and several other key people make Trump possible. Without them Trump wouldn't be and couldn't be Trump. You will find this "theme" true of all incredibly accomplished, successful, and wealthy entrepreneurs.

In short, the people around you, the people who populate your world, the people you rely on either enhance or sap your wealth attraction power. No person with whom you interact is a neutral factor. Each and every person either drains power from you or contributes power to you. One or the other. Power source or power drain. Ally or enemy. Black or white.

Refusing to face the black-and-white nature of this, with clarity and accuracy and honesty, is a major obstacle to wealth attraction. Refusing to act appropriately and decisively about what you deduce about a person, about a power drainer, is a major obstacle to wealth attraction.

How To Build a "Power Team" Around You

I have been very, very fortunate in my life to have had a number of people around me who have added to my power. They have changed over time, some left, some came. Change is inevitable. But I have certainly had an enormous amount of support.

Mine is in tiers.

In the first tier have been spouses, close associates, close friends, people I've relied on heavily, at different times, in different ways. My second wife, Carla, for example, was an important, chief source of support and power for many of the 22 years of our marriage. After a brief divorce, we are re-married and, in different ways than before, she is a greater source of support than ever before. At present, Bill Glazer, who publishes my *No B.S. Marketing Letter,* is President of Glazer-Kennedy Insider's Circle™ and his crackerjack staff, and Pete Lillo, who publishes another of my newsletters, are enormously valuable business associates I can rely on without equivocation. Vicky Tolleson, my lone employee, office manager, personal assistant, time-and-access sentry, problem solver, and client services director, is valuable beyond description. These people and a very short list of others, past or present, work with me pretty much on my terms, with the prime purpose of supporting and facilitating my productivity. They view their responsibility and best interests as making it possible for me to function at peak performance. I also have a very short list of people I can rely on for advice, counsel, information. It features Lee Milteer, a close friend and associate, who is a reliable sounding board, encourager but also questioner. The total number of people in this tier, at any given time, is less than a dozen.

In the second tier are both suppliers and clients. For example, for 11 years, I've run a formal "mastermind group" exclusively for information marketers in business akin to my own, all highly successful and innovative, all wealthy. While they pay me well to organize, host, facilitate, and direct the group and its meetings, I also participate as a member and benefit from the exchange of ideas and information. This tier also includes my CPA firm, the person I am most involved with in real estate investments, Darin Garman, and other paid advisors.

In the third tier are all the other clients I work with, the other vendors I rely on, the other sources of information I access, trade associations I belong to. Included here, for example, is the publisher of this book, its editor, its marketing people, my other publishers, my literary agents, my publicist. Also included are my consulting and copywriting clients who I work for and who support me, but toward whom I must still act discriminately. Also included, editors, graphic artists, web masters, other professionals and vendors I use intermittently, project by project.

This is "Planet Dan," a world I create and own and control, populated only by people I permit to be there, governed by laws I legislate and enforce. It's a small planet, so I have some level of personal relationship with every inhabitant of the planet. Everyone of these relationships is a two-way street. They all influence me as I influence them. That's unavoidable. They all either enhance or drain my energy. They all either support and facilitate or interfere with my productivity. They all either enhance or disrupt my wealth attraction.

This is true of every single person you permit existence in your world, too. Rule *your* world accordingly.

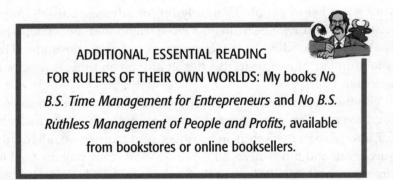

ADDITIONAL, ESSENTIAL READING
FOR RULERS OF THEIR OWN WORLDS: My books *No B.S. Time Management for Entrepreneurs* and *No B.S. Ruthless Management of People and Profits*, available from bookstores or online booksellers.

Wealth Magnet 27
Courage

I have an unpublished book I've been working on, off and on, for years with the words "brass balls" in its title. The publishers I've approached lack the brass balls to publish it! You can, however, get the gist of its 300-page message just from those two words. The meek may inherit the earth, but not anytime soon. **Fortune favors the bold. Courage attracts wealth.**

You have to put yourself out there.

I'm not talking about taking unbridled financial risk, although from time to time, you do have to put some chips on the table. This is about your ego, self-esteem, reputation, relationships, dealing with the ever-present *"what will he/she/they think of me?"*

You need courage to act on your ideas. Courage to defy conventional wisdom or even the expert advice you solicit when you believe best. Courage to start before you are ready, to fumble

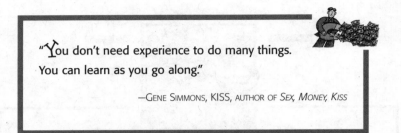

> "You don't need experience to do many things. You can learn as you go along."
>
> —GENE SIMMONS, KISS, AUTHOR OF *SEX, MONEY, KISS*

around in the dark, screw up. Courage to face embarrassment, humiliation, rejection. Courage to stand by your convictions. Courage to make demands, set rules and boundaries, define the way you will do business, impose your will on the world around you. Courage to end unproductive relationships, fire uncooperative employees or clients. Courage to wrest control of your time from everyone around you. Courage to define and pursue goals. Courage to ask, promote, sell aggressively, forcefully, noisily, visibly. Courage to ignore criticism and to focus on results.

Wealth rarely rewards wimps.

In an ethereal sense, I think wealth is waiting, watching the entrepreneur, holding back a while, just to see how big and brassy his balls are—or how small and dull. (And to be gender sensitive, I want to mention that two female fans of mine, both highly successful entrepreneurs, created a company called Women With Balls as paean to this idea.) At some point, wealth's admiration, even lust for the incredibly strong, certain, unwavering, resilient entrepreneur boils over and wealth comes running toward the entrepreneur, wealth gives herself up totally and completely. (Need a cold shower?)

There are very real forces that govern the movement of money. Money doesn't move around from one person to another, by fate, accident, luck. It moves for reasons, in response to magnetic forces. Money moves because of Authority—that's why experts get rich, why the top cardiac surgeon at Cleveland Clinic is so much wealthier than the generalist M.D. just down the street. Money moves with Transfer of Responsibility—that's how financial planners and advisors, brokers, and money managers get rich. Money moves on a base level because of Value Exchange. But most of all, it is my understanding that money moves because of Courage.

Wealth Magnet 28
Pace

I f you do not live in New York City, when you visit, you will very quickly notice that the entire city is vibrating at high energy and in motion at a very different pace than just about anywhere else you've ever been. It is so relentlessly intense that New York businesspeople must engineer frequent weekend and summer escapes to avoid completely burning out. In Las Vegas, big-time casinos like Caesars Palace have a different pace on Friday and Saturday nights than on week nights or afternoons and it definitely influences peoples' behavior and how they part with their money. People who've hung around and observed me at work, in my regular work environment, or on a TV infomercial set or at a multi-day conference, have often commented on observing a distinct difference in pace than they've been accustomed to. At Disney World, they have a little trick of altering the pace of the background music playing throughout the park as closing time approaches, to re-energize the weary and move them toward the exits more quickly. Competitors on Donald Trump's *Apprentice* and *Celebrity Apprentice* television shows have told me the difference between surviving and leaving early, between winning and losing, had as much to do with being able to handle the intense pressure and fast pace of unfolding events as it did anything else.

These are all examples of pace at work.

Pace is not simple speed. In the horse racing in which I'm engaged, for example, the outright fastest horse wins fewer than 30% of the races. Instead, it's up to the driver to pace the race, buy his horse millisecond breathers and rests, if leading, to regulate the pace of the race so he has some gas left in the tank for the stretch drive. But pace is about speed a lot, too, and The New Economy is very, very intolerant of the slow. We live in a now-time world, people consumed by connectivity, instant communication, news known as it occurs or mere minutes later, and constant change in just about every field of endeavor. In business, what's called speed-to-market in corporate circles has never been more important.

As there is a certain rhythm to the city of New York or to interacting most effectively with thousands of attendees at a conference and to the conference itself or to a horse race, there is a winning rhythm to sales, negotiation, alchemizing ideas, launching products, business operations, and attracting money. I have thought about this a great deal and wound up unable to break it down and teach it like dance steps, 1–2–3 cha–cha–cha, quarter turn left. I'm afraid it's more like *innate* rhythm—you either got it or you don't.

If that's the case, why even mention it in this book?

Because it plays such a big role it is out of integrity to omit it.

There is, for example, a rhythm to successful deal-making. You need a certain level of speed and momentum from start to finish. Not reckless or desperate speed, but a pace that builds on itself

"*There's a kind of rhythm to making money that something inside me responds to.*"

and creates enthusiasm for getting the deal done and moving onto implementation. If you do deals, you feel it. Or you don't, and when you don't, you know there's trouble. I'm betting every good deal-maker has this same sensation and works at creating it, but probably can't lay it out in steps any better than I can.

Here's something even more bizarre to most: I actually *feel* money coming to me before it arrives. I know within the first hour or so if today is going to be "a money day" or not, regardless of what activities are scheduled. As example, a day not too long ago brought a prospective client I'd met with over a year ago and forgotten about back to the table, seemingly "out of the blue," now ready to start a project paying me over $100,000.00. After receiving the fax, I realized I'd had that tingling sensation all morning but had nothing on the books that day to warrant any expectation of directly making or receiving money.

The flip of this is the more of that feeling I can create, the more money is attracted to me. One of the ways I create that feeling is by pace. By picking up the pace of work, for example, I find I not only get more done and move projects and people forward faster, but I create a special kind of kinetic energy that is exceptionally attractive to money.

I watch a lot of people drain all the energy out of a good idea or a promising deal with slow and steady and methodical pace. Details that can easily be resolved later or, even if difficult, would be resolved later by people already in the soup together become obsessed over and turn into insurmountable, opportunity-killing obstacles before they ever need to be confronted. For me, and most wealthy entrepreneurs I know, success is cooked in messy kitchens. Ingredients on hand are substituted because no shopping list was meticulously made. Some yelling and cleaver waving may go on. It's all part of the pace of high performance and major accomplishment. If you slow things down to prevent every problem in advance, you risk everything stopping altogether.

One application of this, that I talk a lot about in my Renegade Millionaire System, is: simultaneous, not sequential. Using deal-making again as example, one I put together for a client, getting his company access to a bigger competitors' customer lists via three joint venture marketing campaigns, offered a million dollars or more in profit via customers moved from them to him for unlimited future use, but I had no idea which of the three projects would prove fruitful, which would disappoint the joint venture partner profoundly. I structured the deal for all three to move forward and be implemented simultaneously for that very reason. Literally, one campaign would work its way through their lists Z to A over a few weeks while another traveled A to Z those same weeks and the third overlapped the other two. I also got the deal in place quickly from first tentative conversation to done by hopping on a jet and flying there, then handing it off with a timetable agreed to in principle, that would lead to very quick implementation, a pace intended to prevent re-thinking and equivocation. Sadly, the client engaged in timidity, and converted this to sequential rather than simultaneous, easily getting the other party to welcome a more prudent and methodical approach, testing one campaign at a time, with time in between each to assess results. Worse, the speed of implementation of the first went from weeks to months. You can predict the outcome without me finishing the paragraph. The first initiative produced minimum, disappointing results, everything else was scuttled, the relationship fizzled, the opportunity died. In reality, it was still-born.

Presented with a very similar situation more recently, I kept control, set multiple new initiatives moving forward at fast pace, and will be just fine if only one works out as intended. Incidentally, as a very nitty-gritty detail insight, let me tell you how I moved that negotiation forward over just a few days, without violating the sanctity of my work regimen of limited access and control of clients including never taking unscheduled incoming calls and playing phone tag. On three occasions, I faxed additional information and suggestions, then gently dictated the time of a phone call the next day, indicating in the fax that I would have a brief window, from, for example, 1:00 P.M. to 2:30 P.M., and would call and try and connect several times during that window, but would not be accessible for return calls. On each occasion, guess what? The CEO was right there, on the dot, waiting for my call. As I said, the winning driver, if leading the race, must control its pace.

When I said earlier that the rhythm of this seems innate, and that you've either got it or you haven't, you may have thought

"Well, I don't have it and that's that." I think that over-simplifies and too easily disqualifies. If you consult dictionary and the-saurus, you'll find that innate does mean inborn, natural, and unlearned. But it also means instinctive, intuitive, and hard-wired. Experts in intuitiveness—from the famous Amazing Kreskin to more serious psychologists and academics—believe that most people have more intuitive powers than they realize or let themselves use. If you look at the work of Dr. Sidis, Dr. Edward Kramer, to some extent Montessori, you'll find the belief that education engineered as a stuffing in of information and skill is a narrow view. Instead, their belief is that we are born with an enormous range of innate intelligence and the role of education should be to draw it out of us and empower us to access and use it. The word "educate" has Latin roots, *educat* and *educere*, which translate as led out and lead out—not stuff in. Finally, if your spiritual beliefs include a beneficent God, then you have to believe you are hard-wired to attract prosperity. All this suggests to me that, while you can't learn the pace of wealth attraction like you might learn dance steps or installing a toilet, you already possess this innate intelligence and need only let it emerge from within and begin working for you. This is, I believe, facilitated by actively working on and with all the other Wealth Magnets contained in this book. In concert, they create an envi-ronment conducive to this pace.

As an analogy, consider another power; the power of acute observation. The enduringly popular fictional detective Sherlock Holmes was able to make extraordinary deductions primarily by observing what others could have but did not. His mind was conditioned to take note of minute detail. The details were there for anyone to see. The ability to do so is very likely innate intel-ligence we all possess. The currently popular television program *The Mentalist* on CBS features a Holmsien main character, who has come, by his exceptional observatory powers, from a life as a charlatan mind reader. Truly extraordinary face-to-face sales pro-fessionals exhibit and rely on being able to "read people" in large part by observing a myriad of little details in their dress, demeanor, speech and language, body language, physical environment. I've seen people go from being utterly tone deaf in this way to very adept as a result of becoming employed in selling, without ever getting force-fed education or training about it, through experience—but that experience is really the placing of themselves in an environment conducive to and demanding of them letting this innate intelligence awaken and rise up out of their own subconscious.

In short, there's hope. There's reason to expect yourself to grow more and more adept, naturally adept, automatically functioning at creating the pace of wealth attraction.

No Waiting

Walt Disney started the company that became Disney as we know it today just as the Great Depression was about to start— after a previous bankruptcy. W. Clement Stone built his giant Combined Insurance Companies of America out of the Depression. Bill Gates and Paul Allen began Microsoft's march toward world domination in a recession. Bezos launched Amazon—at first named something no one could spell correctly—in a recession. This list is long; of successful companies birthed in sour times, with remarkably poor timing.

Timing definitely matters. The difference between salad and garbage is timing. The market is often ripe for a particular thing after some have tried bringing it forward too early, and before some arrive too late. It is also true that there are times when it is easier to do a thing than at other times. In 2008, for example, merger and acquisition activity was at a five-year low and both capital and financing for deals was held in tight fists; however, the giant Imbev/Anheuser-Busch deal did get done, and at breakneck speed, from start to finish in just 90 days, with the M&A attorneys sleeping on couches at the office and working seven-day weeks. Would it have been easier to do a year or two earlier? Probably. But the players weren't ready then. I suppose it's better to have timing as an ally when and if possible, but that still doesn't often justify waiting for it. Because trying to correctly time timing is as close to impossible as we can get. There is nonsense sold to casino gamblers about trying to time their entry into table games just as they are getting "hot" or to snag a slot machine that has been primed; but every spin and every deal is random and its own event. Investors and speculators who try timing markets and predicting bottoms and tops are invariably slaughtered.

In marketing, timing is often blamed for other sins. Countless products, from pantyhose to weight loss products and skin care for men to pet vitamins were brought to the market and failed dismally and all but disappeared only to re-surface and become immensely popular. Were they at first "before their time" and only later an "idea whose time has come"—thus victims and beneficiaries of timing—or were they at first improperly positioned, poorly marketed, or otherwise handicapped? The trouble with timing is that it is so hard to control. You could put the same product or proposition before me one week and get a "no" and a week earlier or later get a "yes." But how could you know the right week in advance? (This is why the smartest marketers identify a target prospect group in which

"The Only Time Is NOW Time"

—Dr. Edward Kramer

everyone will be ripe at some point, and there is sufficient value to justify being omnipresent.)

Ultimately, most who attract wealth seem to plow ahead regardless of the conditions and circumstances they must plow *through*, helped at times by fortuitous timing but refusing to be hindered by disadvantageous timing. Had Disney or Stone or Gates or Bezos heeded wise counsel, erred on the side of caution, and waited for better times, would we still have the empire of the Mouse on which the sun never sets? Would Stone have ever built his company and still become a billionaire? Would we still be enslaved by Microsoft? Would we still all be buying from Amazon? I don't know, I can't guess, and there's no way for anyone else to know either. But for the most part, it's not what wealth attractors usually do, so it's not the kind of question they ever ponder. They are busy doing, while others are pondering.

In many ways, timing has recently seemed unfavorable for so many things, yet I'm certain that a decade from now, there'll be a Disney and a Stone and a Gates with stories to tell of starting something when everyone advised them not to, when every hill seemed steep, when every door seemed closed, at this time, right now. Because it's never the person who catalogs all the reasons not to who winds up in front or at the top or glorified in the media or getting a suntan on the deck of his yacht. It's really quite difficult to tell the difference between brazen and reckless and reasonably prudent and cautious and over-timid and intimidated. That's why getting it right pays so well. Because it's difficult.

Reprinted from The No B.S. MARKETING GOLD LETTER, supplement to No B.S. MARKETING LETTER published by Glazer-Kennedy Insider's Circle™, www.DanKennedy.com.

BONUS CHAPTERS
Examples of
Wealth Attraction in Action

How a Small University
Went from Stodgy to
Spectacular using Wealth
Attraction Magnets

I am pleased to hold a position on the advisory board of the School of Communication at High Point University. Its president, Dr. Nido R. Qubein, has been a friend for many years, has, at my invitation, addressed Glazer-Kennedy Insider's Circle™ events and conferences, and we have done business together on occasion over the years. His life is a classic American success story, having raised himself from empty-pockets immigrant with nominal grasp of the English language to highly paid professional speaker, sought-after consultant, member of boards of companies like Great Harvest Bread Company and La-Z-Boy, founder of a bank, and philanthropist. But nothing on his resume even approaches the magnitude of all he has accomplished at dizzying speed in the total transformation of High Point University. To protect him from the wrath of his academic peers,

let me quickly say he would not approve of my "stodgy to spectacular" description. It is mine and mine alone. It is accurate. In
short order, as this chapter will partially describe, he has re-made
the university in every imaginable and many unimaginable
ways. If the Disney Imagineers were to create a college, they
couldn't top this.

Before you hear from Donald Scarborough, Ed.D., Vice-
President for Institutional Advancement at High Point University,
I have just a few things I want to say.

I urge, urge, urge visiting HighPoint.edu to see as much as
can be seen of this amazing place online. If your travels take you
anywhere near High Point, North Carolina, go in person, tour,
observe. Nothing read or seen at distance can do this remarkable
place justice. Beyond being an outstanding academic institution,
it is a living, breathing, thriving demonstration of wealth attraction. It will inspire you to create more exceptional experiences for
your own clientele—and show you how to do it. As you will
soon discover, this university has its own Director of WOW!, its
own concierge service, and, of course, its own Starbucks. Dig
deeper, though, and you will discover an attention to micro-
detail bordering on obsessive and a Disney-like creativity and
flexibility and responsiveness you rarely find alive anywhere, let
alone at a college. To that point, here's a story from the book
*Insider Secrets To Delivering Red Carpet Service: The Celebrity
Experience* by Donna Cutting, from her visit to HPU:

> *President Qubein has made it a habit to walk around the HPU
> campus with his leadership team on a regular basis. While on
> one of these walks, he noticed a path that students had made
> through the grass to get to one of the buildings instead of using
> the beautiful brick walkways that had been provided for them.
> He asked his maintenance team about it, and their response
> was that they had tried pleading, cajoling, erecting signs,
> everything they could think of to keep the students from walk-
> ing on the grass—nothing had worked. "What ideas do you*

have?" they asked their new president. The answer he gave sur-
prised them. "Get a bricklayer over here and make a new path
over the one the students have made." Nido realized that the
students knew the path through the grass was the shortest dis-
tance from point A to point B. Of course they wanted to cut
through the grass! So he took a cue from his customer. He
began to look for other places where students had made their
own paths to get where they were going, and he put brick walk-
ways in those very spots.

What do you think of that? I see my Wealth Magnet 17, See
What Isn't There, and Wealth Magnet 10, Do Something, in play.
Welcome to The New Economy, where finding ways to respond
to and enhance the customer experience whenever possible is
paramount, and decisiveness and speed of equal criticality.

You might think this contrary to my insistence that businesses be designed to serve their owners' preferences. It is not. On
things that really matter to you—say, hours worked or how you
are accessible to customers, for example—you should seek ways
to attract clientele who are not at odds with you, train customers
to do business with you as you want them to, and offer compen-
sating benefits you don't mind giving. And business owners do
routinely underestimate their own latitude in such matters. But
something like the location of the brick paths has no real importance to Nido. Why be stubborn about *it?* Almost every other
university president would be. The grounds crew was. Why not,
instead, make changes that make customers happier? Leadership
involves discretion; picking battles, not making everything a bat-
tle. And seizing opportunities. Most business owners are the
opposite of Nido; they have their rule books in hand, heels dug
in, eyes closed tight. They are all about keeping those darned
customers off the grass! No sane businessperson believes the customer is always right, but we should be willing to admit that
sometimes the customer has better ideas—and we should be out
walking around looking for them.

HOW A SMALL UNIVERSITY WENT FROM STODGY TO SPECTACULAR USING WEALTH-ATTRACTION MAGNETS

My own visits to HPU, my own walking around with Nido have revealed many situations quite similar to the brick paths, and a consistent way in which he responds to them—creatively.

Now, for the rest of this story . . . .

🦋 🦋 🦋

The Renaissance at High Point

By Donald A. Scarborough, Ed.D.

During the fall semester of 2004, HPU's president announced his retirement. The University had been established in 1924 and is located in High Point, North Carolina—"The Furniture Capital of the World." Soon a search for a new leader began. Quickly the Search Committee turned to one of its own members, Dr. Nido R. Qubein. Dr. Qubein had a professional speaking schedule second to none, he consulted with numerous major national and international corporations, and he was the owner of several other companies while serving as a director on many others. After responding "no" on several occasions, he prayerfully considered the opportunity and resolved that it would a good time to pay back his adopted country and his *alma mater* for the success he had achieved. So, he decided to accept the role for a few years in order to get the University back on a sound footing—raise some money, organize the business functions, recruit a leadership team, etc. Little did he know that he would fall in love with the students, own the purpose, and adopt a mission to totally and completely rethink and retool High Point University.

Wealth Magnets 2, 5, 10, 14, 17, 23 and 27

Dr. Qubein became HPU's seventh president on January 1, 2005. He knew that the University needed a significant kick start. With strong confidence and exuberance, he set a bold *fundraising goal of $10 million from friends and supporters of the University in his first month at work*—it turned out to be $21 million in only 21 days on

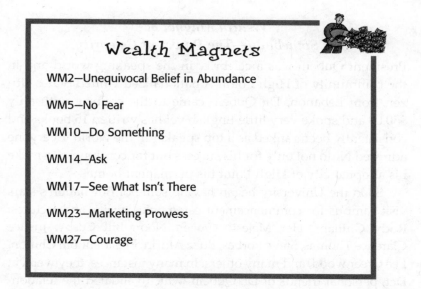

Wealth Magnets

WM2—Unequivocal Belief in Abundance

WM5—No Fear

WM10—Do Something

WM14—Ask

WM17—See What Isn't There

WM23—Marketing Prowess

WM27—Courage

the job. The confidence and determination he displayed "infected" everyone he approached.

Since then, the unimaginable transformation touches every aspect of the University—an educational, physical, and environmental metamorphosis. The results garnered national acclaim—*U.S. News and World Report's* "America's Best Colleges" 2009 edition ranks HPU at No. 1 among "Up-and-Coming Schools" and No. 5 among all comprehensive colleges in the Southern United States. Current and prospective students and parents and the University's family rallied in support of their University, now considered by many an educational model.

Alumni, friends, and supporters have donated more than $112 million without a formal capital campaign. The HPU family captured President Qubein's confidence and vision, and support has been widespread. In June 2008, HPU received a standalone credit rating of A– from Standard & Poor's based on "headcount, solid student demand characteristics, strong financial operations, impressive short-term fund raising, and strong leadership and management."

Wealth Magnet 8:
Be Somebody—The Power of Celebrity

President Qubein was a celebrity in the speaking world and in the community of High Point. A nationalized United States citizen from Lebanon, Dr. Qubein came to the country with only $50.00 and spoke very little English yet has written 15 books and consistently been ranked as a top speaker in the world. Everyone admired Nido not only for his success but for continuing to make his adopted city of High Point his permanent home.

Soon the University began having some of our nation's stars visit campus for commencement ceremonies, visits, and lectures: Rudy Giuliani, Her Majesty Queen Noor, Bill Cosby, Justice Clarence Thomas, Steve Forbes, Buzz Aldrin, President Bill Clinton, Lee Greenwood, and many others. In many instances, they were, in fact, personal friends of Dr. Qubein, which validated the relationship and purpose of their visits. These nationally known individuals were soon blown away by the renaissance of High Point University under President Qubein's leadership.

Wealth Magnet 17:
See What Isn't There

When President Qubein started he found an enrollment of 1,492 undergraduate students. Over and over again, he told faculty, friends, supporters, everybody, "We have thrown the box out of the window of the train that has already left the station!" Every decision process was given the freedom to reach for new horizons to recommend only the best alternative. In four academic years, 2,700 (+81%) undergraduate students (2,450 [+61%] residential students) attend with an average SAT score increase of over 70 points. Freshman enrollment alone has grown from 2005's 370 students to 1040 in August 2009—an increase of 181%. Current students come from more than 50 countries and 40 states. By 2011, HPU's enrollment will approach 5,000 students—3,400 undergraduates (2,800 residential) and 1,500 graduate and evening students.

The University employs a Director of WOW!—developing "WOWs" while eliminating "unWOWs." The campus concierge is a one-stop service center—wake-up calls, maintenance issues, dinner reservations, dry cleaning, and more. The cafeteria has live music daily, kiosks dispense snacks each morning, an ice cream truck roams the campus, and nightly valet parking is provided. Student birthdays are a big event—a card and a Starbucks giftcard from President Qubein, balloons, a special meal prepared by the campus chef. Even faculty and staff members receive birthday calls from the president. These personal touches undergird HPU's caring campus community.

HPU's transformation under President Qubein's guidance is now driven by a $300-million investment in capital improvements: 7 buildings demolished, 27 other structures renovated completely, 18 new ones built, and 2 buildings currently under construction or design. By August 2009, five new residence halls will have added 1,500 beds. In total, over 1-million square feet of building space has been added to the campus. The $62-million University Center (277,000 square feet), opened August 2009, containing student housing, movie theater, study areas, entertainment venues, and multiple dining options (including a steakhouse!). The campus has grown by 60 acres to the current 180 acres [+200%].

Wealth Magnet 23: Superentrepreneurs Are Unabashed, Unashamed, Irrepressible Promoters

The University did not turn to some outside/unknown marketing company; it turned to the administrative staff. They personally took charge of telling the HPU story. These leaders understood that the "family" needed a clear understanding of the University before they could convince others. Initially, the marketing reached out to the entire community of High Point's students, faculty, friends, staff, trustees, etc. who may have been a part of the University for most of their lives but were not able to tell a central story. So, a picture began to be painted that everyone understood of a treasure that most had always taken for granted. Soon, everywhere you looked on campus you saw "HPU" or "High Point University"—High Point University window stickers soon appeared on every employee's automobile. For the local community, the University has now become known as "High Point's University." What emerged was a wide range of individuals who could describe the University in very similar terms no matter who was telling the story, which created an authenticity that had never before existed.

From the campus, the marketing campaigns moved to the Triad of North Carolina (High Point, Greensboro, and Winston-Salem) and then across the State of North Carolina. One story was told to me by a parent of a prospective student who was visiting the campus for a weekend with hundreds of others competing in a major academic scholarship program. The mother told me that their flight from Maine had been delayed, and they were afraid that they were going to be late arriving at the University.

Once they arrived at the Greensboro Airport, the mother started frantically trying to find out how she was going to find her way to High Point University. Then, her daughter tapped her on the shoulder and told her mom to just calm down and relax. The daughter said, "Mom, don't worry. I think they own the airport!" As she lifted her head going down the escalator to pick up her bags, she found herself totally surrounded by High Point University's campus. "I thought that I was already on the University's International Promenade!"

Dr. Qubein then altered the focus of his professional speaking presentations where business and decision makers came together for him to be their teacher. He continued to speak about serious marketing and business practices that are essential for businesses around the country. However, he demonstrated the positive impact achieved by these principles by the successes realized on the HPU campus. Immediately the attendees were so enthralled that they began sending their sons and daughters from across the country to HPU as students. Soon, the media took note and the University began receiving time on nationally syndicated radio talk shows; the national television networks took notice, too. ABC, CBS, and NBC have featured HPU's commencement speakers on their annual college and university commencement overview in May of each year. ABC's *Good Morning America Weekend* edition featured HPU's unique approach to customer service with the students and their families. Now, these types of local, regional, and national exposures occur frequently.

Dr. Qubein and his staff intimately knew the HPU campus, its history, its clients, its opportunities, and their own experiences quickly translated them into a successful market strategy that resonated with others.

"At High Point University, Every Student Receives an Extraordinary Education, in a Fun Environment, with Caring People"

Slane Student Activity and Fitness Center: 90,000 square feet of space, which is a definitive center of activity for HPU students. Originally built in 1972 and renovated in 2007, some of the amenities include a 450-seat cafeteria, post office, book-store, study lounges, recreation areas, meeting rooms, basketball courts, aerobics room, lockers, and a food court, which includes a Starbucks.

The social environment compliments the total development of the HPU student, yet a strong academic environment remains the core of any outstanding University. As the University's motto acclaims, HPU centers on an extraordinary academic and social environment. A 14:1 student-to-faculty ratio highlights the University's focus on providing the optimum educational environment. The faculty has grown by 27% since 2005, adding a total of 58 new members in the 2008–09 and 2009–10 academic years. Along with classroom technology, each academic building houses designated study areas. Since the library (open 24/7) renovation, student usage has increased 25 percent. Likewise, residence halls contain dedicated study areas and business centers.

"HPU is no ordinary University, and that's why I love it so much," said sophomore Chelsea Johnson. "When you're here, you realize that there is so much more making you go 'Wow!'" "That's the point," says President Qubein. "When you focus on the total student experience, they love it. And, when they love it, they reward us in the classroom. My message to students is very balanced. There's a time to play and a time to study. There is a time to be in the classroom and be attentive." At High Point University, much has occurred during the past four academic years. The transformation continues at lightning speed—an unending process.

Chapter courtesy High Point University, High Point, North Carolina. Online at HighPoint.edu.

The Reinvention of the
Barbershop with Wealth
Attraction

O n one level, could there be a more ordinary, run-
of-the-mill, mundane, and commoditized business than
men's haircuts? And how on earth could such a business
be made a beacon of creativity magnetic to money?

Briefly in this book I alluded to the enormity of the opportunity in creating and delivering exceptional experience-based
products and services to the mass-affluent and affluent markets.
In another book in this series, *No B.S. Marketing to the Affluent*, I
deal with the subject extensively. It is my contention that the best
place to attract wealth is a place where there is wealth. It's not
much harder but it can be much more rewarding to aim your
business at the upper echelons than at the bottom. But when you
do, the business must be about something more than its core
goods and services.

This is what attracted me to the business that became Kennedy's All-American Barber Club®, although my name in its name is mostly coincidental, only a tiny bit ceremonial honor; I am a founding investor as well as marketing strategy advisor, but I have no managerial role, responsibility, or control. The owners *claim* they were thinking of other Kennedys when choosing the name. In any case, my enthusiasm is entirely based on this as a perfect example of a New Economy Business utilizing a wide range of my wealth attraction principles as well as my marketing strategies. It has and champions a philosophy, strives for emotional connection, is for a particular customer, and is about more than its core deliverable; a shave and a haircut. Its CEO, Chris Hurn, describes how he sees it fit into the Wealth Attraction Magnets you've been reading about in this book, on the following pages. Before ceding to him, I'll make two points of my own about this business concept:

One of the strategic marketing changes that I've been urging on my clients as they move into The New Economy, is called "chore to more." It means transforming what is, for most customers, a chore, at best bothersome, at worst unpleasant, into something more. More enjoyable, more gratifying, more interesting—or, if none of those seem possible, at least more convenient and efficient. High-end supermarkets have moved in this creative direction, adding good on-site child care facilities, cafés, even day-spas, so the girls can meet at the market, drop off their kids, and make a day of it—and they do. It's my opinion every business needs to follow their lead. For most guys, getting their hair cut is a boring chore they put off. It is an inconvenient time-suck, it sends them into environments they aren't comfortable in, and it is utterly uninteresting. Some shops have tried mitigating this by slapping a few flat-screen TV's up on the wall tuned to sports channels, but this isn't fooling anybody—it's like playing a Disney music CD real loud while you clean out the garage or pick up dog poop in the backyard and trying to convince yourself you're having fun. C'mon. I'm not talking about putting prettier wallpaper over top of a battered, moldy wall; I'm talking about replacing the old with new and different. Kennedy's is definitely a "chore-to-more" business.

The other point has to do with the business from the owner-ship standpoint. Many, many successful small-business owners, professionals in private practice like doctors, dentists, account-ants, financial advisors, traveling sales professionals, and others can benefit enormously from owning a second business. While their first business or career takes care of their current financial needs and desires, pays off the mortgage, and sends the kids to college, the second business can pour all its take-home profits into wealth-building and retirement funds. This is the only prac-tical way for many to have the option of retiring early, and to retire rich. But most businesses, franchised or not, are too compli-cated, too costly, and too time-demanding to meet this need. The leadership team at Kennedy's deliberately designed a small foot-print, easy to manage and absentee manage, high-profit, stable income business with this unique type of franchise owner in mind. Consequently, almost all franchisees to date have other, successful businesses or careers and are developing their Kennedy's Barber Clubs as second businesses. This has Kennedy's aimed at a very different potential franchisee candi-date than 95% of all other franchisors. This is Wealth Magnet 17—Seeing What Isn't There—deployed in a very practical way.

To attract wealth in The New Economy, I think you have to be different than others, do things differently than others, and pursue different people than the majority of those categorized as your competitors are pursuing. The business to which you'll be introduced in this chapter embodies all three of these maneuvers. I also urge you to visit KennedysBarberClub.com for a more in-depth look.

Shave and a Haircut, Not Two Bits

By Chris Hurn

My name is Chris Hurn. I'm in Dan's Platinum Mastermind Group and am the Independent Business Advisor (Chapter Director for Glazer-Kennedy Insider's Circle™) in Orlando, Florida. I'm also a bit of a serial entrepreneur and investor. Among the five businesses I run are an *Inc.* 500-honored commercial finance company (Mercantile Capital Corporation), a strategic marketing consulting and business coaching firm (Hurn, Harter and Worrall), and my latest, a national franchise. This franchise, where I'm both the Franchisor and a Franchisee, is called Kennedy's All-American Barber Club® (*and no, the name was not chosen in relation to Dan*).

Kennedy's is a mass-affluent-targeted, membership-based, classic barbershop concept that stands in contrast to everything else in this space. As of this writing, there are six Clubs open and another 51 already sold and to be developed over the next five years. This is in only the first year. Even in the "strained" economic times in which we started out, we are rapidly building-out this unique concept nationally, with individual unit and master territory franchisees. More importantly, the Clubs we have opened are all showing tremendous growth, and that's a testament to our business model, the selection of our ideal clients, and our continued execution of our systems.

Dan asked me to relate some of the Wealth Magnets in this book to Kennedy's, as an example of how a very purposefully created business utilizes the principles herein. While we employ all of the Wealth Magnets to varying degrees, some in particular stand out.

Wealth Magnet 1: No Guilt

Life is to be lived. Abundance is all around us. And we should partake in most of the pleasures of this world. Those are key beliefs we hold at Kennedy's. Yes, our barbershop franchise has *beliefs* because we're not really in the barbershop business; we're in the "movement" business . . . but more on that later.

Kennedy's is built on the premise that the modern man could use a little pampering, that it's OK for him to indulge a bit. Now, this isn't an idea with which many men are overly comfortable (*although the ranks are growing by the hour*), nor are most typically seeking this, at least consciously, for whatever reasons. In my experience, men are often dragged to a spa with their significant other, but once there, they tend to enjoy it—quite a bit. In fact, men's spa services and men's grooming product sales are the fastest areas of growth in their respective niches.

Philosophically, we believe our clients deserve a little pampering now and again, and we're here to provide it. Men throughout the ages have gone to their neighborhood barbershops to "clean up" and in so doing, have generally had a pleasant experience. Unfortunately for Modern Man, the unisex movement of the 1970s all but killed off the American barbershop, as we'd come to know it. Kennedy's represents us bringing back something quite unique and nostalgic, but with a modern twist of new improvements.

In saying that they "deserve it," we at Kennedy's are exhibiting the "No Guilt" Wealth Magnet. I've often told potential franchisees that Kennedy's is in the "small indulgences" business and in the "affordable luxury" realm. Our clients typically work hard—often carrying the proverbial "weight of the world" on their shoulders—and they shouldn't feel ashamed of becoming well groomed and receiving a little exceptional pampering in the process. In fact, it used to be a rite of passage—getting a fresh haircut and a relaxing shave—where men would go celebrate their wins and/or get ready to tackle life. Knights, officers, cowboys, outlaws, statesmen, mobsters, business leaders, sports stars, and celebrities alike would indulge in this practice (*there's a very understandable, yet primitive reason, our clients feel like a king or a kingpin when in our barber chairs*). And we are unapologetic about men deserving this.

Sure, they *could* go to just another, ordinary hair-care place, but why would they? Kennedy's is so much more than just a place to get a haircut and an old-fashioned straight-razor shave (a complimentary beverage—even premium beer!—shoulder massage, shoe-shine, lifestyle magazine, shampoo, and conditioning scalp massage are all standard). That "more" is part of what makes us so special and is one of our core differentiators as a business. But none of our clients should feel guilty because they receive award-winning and luxurious service. I tell our Barbers and Club Managers that it's our honor and privilege to care for our clients in this way. We could provide less, but why would we? Our clients shouldn't have to settle for less. Being "All-American" means living Large, fully appreciating life. Anything less, as the old commercials say, would be uncivilized.

Wealth Magnet 8: Be Somebody

We named our franchise "Kennedy's" because we felt that name represented many good things to many different people—practically all of them being upscale, elite, and enduring. For whatever reasons (*this is not a sociologist's book, so we won't explore them here*), our culture is very clearly obsessed with celebrities. And, given the chance, most people would love to be one themselves.

Whatever your politics, it is undeniable that our 35th President, JFK, was our most handsome, most stylish, and as we've come to learn over the years, a real "ladies man." He was our first "celebrity" President and even presided over our own version of "Camelot." He rubbed elbows with the sports, musical, and movie stars of his era, all while looking completely at ease doing so. I think you'd be hard-pressed to find a modern man who wouldn't have wanted to trade places with him for a little while (*sans the bad back, missile crisis, and assassination*).

Thus, we've come to describe our ideal client as a "Kennedy." For us, it's become a living metaphor. "He's a Kennedy's man alright." "Why don't you just act like a Kennedy, will ya?" "The ladies all look at him as a real Kennedy's man."

For some of our clients, we provide a brief escape into Walter Mitty-like fantasies. Our concept tends to enable them to become somebody they may not really be, even if just for an hour or so. Feeling like you're being treated as James Bond would be or like you're Robert DeNiro playing Al Capone in *The Untouchables* (when reporters encircled him at his knee while he's in his barber chair)—these are the images our clients tell us they feel like when they briefly indulge at a Kennedy's. We allow them to "Be Somebody" they normally aren't or to help build them up into someone they can be.

In doing this, the founders of Kennedy's also demonstrate the "Be Somebody" Wealth Magnet by being the "faces" of the franchise itself. Not only do our pictures and columns appear in every issue of our monthly lifestyle magazine (turning us into mini-celebrities), but we also go to great lengths to live the "Kennedy's" lifestyle in front of our clients and represent the four primary types of men we attract to Kennedy's: business owners; corporate executives; retirees and semi-retirees; and aspiring professionals. We put pictures of us (and our Club Members) with prominent celebrities in our publication, interview celebrities and place them on the covers, and we use examples of celebrities and exclusive settings in our storytelling. All of these associations build up Kennedy's beyond the typical hair care place and into more of a lifestyle movement. WE are "somebodies" and each of our Clients can also "be somebodies" at Kennedy's. Put another way, we created a place where a man can be a man—and these are very few places like that these days.

Wealth Magnet 9: Be Somewhere

This Wealth Magnet is really at the core of the Kennedy's concept. Our clients are typically our Members, as we provide four different membership options to belong to our grooming Clubs, but we also take some walk-in customers. Kennedy's is primarily a place where our clients (Members) belong and that taps into a core psychological need that most men have: to join something; to be a part of something larger than life.

I should also mention that in creating Kennedy's, we were trying to bring back the nostalgic notion of the "gentleman." Somehow over the years, fewer and fewer men describe themselves as or even acting like "gentlemen," yet this very type of man was what made up the "movers and shakers" who helped make America great. A "true" gentlemen's club, as I like to call it (not the perfectly spun misnomer of the strip club variety) a place of fraternity, where likeminded men could come together—that's the type of movement we wanted to create with Kennedy's. In fact, our monthly Kennedy's magazine is even called *The Ultimate Guidebook for the Successful Gentleman*™—and we've been publishing it almost since Day One. This publication telegraphs exactly whom we're trying to attract as Kennedy's men—I call it the "glue" that holds everything together.

Aside from fraternal organizations, which seem to be dying off, no place else quite like Kennedy's exists. Sure, Starbucks may be a "third place," but it doesn't represent anything special for one gender or the other. The town tavern may be a "third place" for some men, but we didn't want to promote *that* particular lifestyle. And while the men's card room at a local country club is getting closer to our ideal, we created Kennedy's as an egalitarian place for all men, be they white collar or blue—to experience the type of exceptional grooming we only used to see in old movies. I like to think we've "democratized" this otherwise elite experience, and several of our more "blue collar" Members have confided in me that Kennedy's is where they treat themselves and where they go to belong on a "different level" (their words, not mine). "Being somewhere" is what Kennedy's means to our Members, and being a Kennedy's man means being seen tackling life. Nothing less will do.

Wealth Magnet 10: Do Something

The notion of the Kennedy's man is one who is "in motion." It's one who is taking action and trying to make a dent in the world. This is a fundamental part of our philosophy and a recurring theme in our monthly lifestyle magazine. As a Club, we want Members who represent certain ideals, and I'd find it hard to call someone a "Kennedy's man" if he wasn't a man of action.

Men tend to like action-movies for the excitement, but also because consciously or subconsciously, we can see ourselves in that movie playing the lead role. At Kennedy's, we help put our Members in that "lead role" of their life—and all they have to do is become a Kennedy's man to become a star in their own right. Since we work on image, confidence, and knowledge in both our Clubs and in our magazines, there simply isn't a good excuse to NOT employ this Wealth Magnet if one is a Kennedy's man in good standing.

Wealth Magnet 13: Integrity

At Kennedy's, our honor is bound by our promises. Our guarantee is, "The Best Haircut and Shave You've Ever Had . . . or it's Free!®" Now, we *know* we have something special at Kennedy's, for I've mystery-shopped our supposed competition all over the country and still haven't found anything I can "borrow" from any of them that beats our 30-step Signature Shave™ process, for instance. So, we're quite certain that the experience we provide is the best our clients will find (*I also haven't found any other barbershops with a guarantee on their service*). We're so sure of it, in fact, that we've guaranteed it and put our money on the line. To me, that's integrity: not only believing you're the best, but doing what it takes to *be* the best, time and again (*excellence for excellence sake*); and then putting it out there as proof, willing to risk something of value if someone so much as *thinks* you're not really the best.

Our reputation is at stake daily at Kennedy's, but we wouldn't be an award-winning barbershop if we didn't act on our superior

procedures and processes. That reliability creates raving fans and helps spur even more "word-of-mouth" advertising for us.

Integrity is a powerful Wealth Magnet . . . and it mostly comes down to doing the "right" thing in business. If you're going to make bold proclamations in business, you better be able to back them up.

Wealth Magnet 17: See What Isn't There

Kennedy's was created to fill the space in the marketplace between the "chop-shops," as we call them, on one side, and the independent barbershops (where you have to worry if the 70-year old barber might cut your ear off due to his diminishing eyesight) on the other. Until Kennedy's came along, most American men reluctantly trudged off to the scissor-wielding sister in the strip-mall who blabs about her ex-boyfriend or baby for the entire 15 minutes of your $15.00 haircut. Pleasurable experience, this was not.

Alternatively, some men still went to the very same barber who remembers putting them in a high-chair to cut their hair.

While Vinny might only charge $10.00 per cut, he more than likely no longer shaves and frills have long since been forgotten.

We knew there had to be a better way—so we created it. Why the old-school barbershop experience had to die with the Rat Pack was beyond us. We wanted to resurrect it. Bring something of quality back. Something that had been so wrongly missing. The opportunity to exploit this underserved market was obvious to me, so we jumped on it.

Having now successfully done this with Kennedy's and continuing to branch-it-out across the country, I've now turned my eye to other "future items" in the Kennedy's arsenal, things that *also* aren't there right now: members-only travel excursions; private-label music, merchandise and beer; and much, much more. These will all be grafted onto our platform, but they also demonstrate that Kennedy's is about much more than just hair, hence the need for philosophies, beliefs, and a point of view.

The key about this Wealth Magnet is not being too far ahead of the "acceptance curve." If you can catch it just right, it can prove to be immensely profitable.

Wealth Magnet 23: Marketing Prowess

Most franchises get their marketing all wrong. I've financed around 45 different franchised concepts over the past dozen years in my commercial lending career, so I've seen a lot of franchised business models; the good, the bad, and the ugly. The commonality among them all is poor marketing. As this isn't necessarily a marketing book, I won't get into too much here (*especially in a Dan Kennedy book*), but suffice to say marketing is one of our greatest strengths at Kennedy's, and it will always be a source of immense wealth for us.

At Kennedy's, we know what our ideal client "looks like," and we know how to market to him, to get him into our Clubs and to try us out. It's as simple as that. Well, truth be told, it's simple on the surface, but very complicated below that. We do LOTS of marketing at Kennedy's to boost our Clubs' memberships quickly, and our marketing serves one purpose and one purpose only: to get that customer to part with his money (on the spot or eventually). Moreover, with our patent-pending membership concept for barbershops, continuity income kicks in from this new Member and, in return, the new Member has the perception of unlimited grooming services.

It took a lot for me, a successful commercial banker, to add to my plate with this franchise, but the economics were too attractive *not* to pounce. There simply isn't a better value proposition (for our Members or our Franchisees) in the hair care business— or to put it another way, we have the best-groomed men in America in our "movement business."

Chris Hurn has appeared numerous times on FOX *Business News* and in such publications as *The Wall Street Journal, The New York Times, USA Today, BusinessWeek, Inc.* magazine,

Entrepreneur magazine, *Forbes*, and *Franchise Times*, as well as in many other regional newspapers and trade journals as the nation's leading expert in small-business lending, franchising, and marketing. Having been in seven business books to date, Chris is also a frequent national speaker, prolific writer, and the recipient of numerous business honors and awards. For more information on Kennedy's All-American Barber Club®, visit: www.KennedysBarberClub.com or call 1-800-31-SHAVE. For more information on Mercantile Capital Corporation, visit: www.TheSmartChoiceLoan.com or call 1-866-MCC-4-504. You can also sign up for Kennedy's magazine, the MCC newsletter, and many other valuable items of interest at those websites.

It's No Wonder
He's So Successful.
Look At . . .

This is the last chapter, the last of the disserta-
tions in these covers on wealth attraction.

I'm about to give you—and then illustrate—an
extra, bonus Wealth Magnet. I didn't number it as one of mine
because it is 100% borrowed from my friend Jim Rohn, perhaps
the pre-eminent success philosopher of our time. Personally, for
the record, I enjoy and am inspired by listening to Jim more than
any other author or speaker whose works I have in my vast
library of audio programs.

One truth of my life that also seems to exist in other wealthy
entrepreneurs' lives is a patchwork piecing together of the philosophy and practical strategies from myriad sources. I don't
think there's any one person who has all the answers anyone
needs. In my case, I can point to three keys developed thanks to

ideas I heard Earl Nightingale advance, one from Jim Rohn—
which I'll tell you about here—a couple from Gary Halbert, one
here, one there, each originating from a different source then validated by many others and ultimately evolved into my own.

The idea Jim Rohn puts forth almost every time he lectures,
which I'd be very remiss if I were to omit it from this book about
attracting wealth, might be described as the whirling dervish
principle. Jim says, if you got an opportunity to shadow any
super-successful person 24/7 for just about any week of their life,
you'd come away from the experience weary and exhausted and
saying to yourself, "Well, it's no wonder he's so successful—look
at *everything* he does." Most people only do a few things to attract
wealth. A handful at most.

Consider Diana Coutu, the pizza entrepreneur I've mentioned
briefly a couple times in this book. In one 60-day period this past
year, here's some of what she did to promote and attract recognition and interest for herself and her business:

- Attended, competed at, and served as a judge at the World
  Pizza Championship Games held in Italy. There, she was
  made an official honorary member of Les Pizziolos du
  France and given a plaque to hang in the pizzeria. None of
  this happened by accident, incidentally; it was the result of
  a great deal of promotion, networking, and effort preced-
  ing the event. Of course, she used all this as fodder for
  news releases to local and national media.
- Appeared on a show on The Food Network.
- Attended the annual HonFest in Baltimore, put on by Café
  Hon, and recognized by *Cosmopolitan* magazine as one of
  the top ten events of the year to attend in the United
  States—and she used this as fodder for publicity, too.
  These same "personal interest stories" made their way to

her Facebook page, her printed newsletter that goes to all her pizzeria's customers as well as a target list of customers-to-be every month, and her websites.

- Was hard at work on her first cookbook, *Passionate About Pizza*, only months from release, for which there will be a promotional blitz to coordinate and execute.
- Began collecting recipes from her customers as well as from celebrities for a second cookbook to quickly follow the first, to be called *Canada's Best Pizzas Cookbook*.
- Developed three new specialty pizzas for promotion for each month.
- Accepted a new post on the Board of Directors of the Canadian Restaurant and Food Association, and went to its meeting in Toronto.
- Provided training, consulting, and coaching to several U.S. restaurant owners on the pizza business.

In the operation of the pizzeria business itself—recently moved to a new location doubled in size—she and her husband Pierre coordinated:

- the launch of a new online ordering system
- a special joint venture promotion giving away a luxury condo vacation in Florida
- a different joint venture promotion for Mother's Day with a local florist.

And there's everything on-going: twice weekly, or more often, e-mails to all the customer-members of their clubs, referral promotion of the month, direct-mail campaigns, new box-stuffer fliers to create, not to mention the on-going training, motivation, and management of staff, product, and delivery quality control, and running of the business. Well, it's no wonder she's so successful—look at *everything* she does!

Diana's available, incidentally, for consulting to those in the restaurant and food service fields, for speaking engagements in and outside of her industry, and at some point, intends franchising Diana's Gourmet Pizzeria. You can contact her at DianasGourmetPizzeria.ca.

● ● ●

Consider my client Michael Gravette. In a short time, he has multiplied a single business into many under the same umbrella. SafetyTechnologies.com was already the largest wholesaler to dealers of personal safety, self-defense, and home security products—from pepper-spray key chains to Tasers to nanny-cams. But in multiplying its size at fast pace, he divided it into one business selling to and supporting retailers like gun shops and professional dealers; a second business putting individuals into the business as independent distributors; then added an in-house website development and hosting service, creating online product catalogs for the re-sellers in both those companies, featuring instant online business set-ups with as many as 200 products, full drop-ship and fulfillment services, and state-of-the-art webstores including secure ordering, e-mail marketing, and video presentations. Nearly simultaneously, he added coaching and training courses for people new to the business as a whole or new to internet marketing. To fuel all this, he coordinates print advertising in over a dozen magazines, direct-mail campaigns to a multitude of lists, e-mail marketing, online article syndication, an online blog, frequently making new videos for the blogs, YouTube and other media, and weekly teleconferences. If that sounds like a full load, wait—there's more! This past year he launched a second sister-business, SafeFamilyLife®, with its own online marketing as well as availability to his existent distributors, to bring a new line of SafeLife Kits to the market, which include some of the Safety Technology products paired with educational manuals, DVDs and audio CDs; for example, The Women's Kit for Personal Safety; The Safe Apartment Living Kit;

The College Survival Kit. This company required development of new products and product packaging, literature, and website development, varied test marketing (some of which failed) and back-to-the-drawing-board re-invention before there was a viable business. Much of this change, improvement, and brand new initiatives took place in 2009–2010, incidentally, against recession headwinds. You can see all this at Safety Technology.com. And it's no wonder he's so successful—look at *everything* he does. Go back and count. Inside what might super-ficially look like one business there are seven businesses in oper-ation, two different salesforces or groups of customers—whichever way you choose to think of them, and nine different, major categories of ongoing activity to bring in business.

In both Diana's and Michael's cases, you have to imagine a very long list of daily Do's, once weekly Do's, and get done by others Do's. If you shadowed either one of them for a week, you'd say "whew." And you would see for yourself the very vis-ible secret of creating a force magnetic to wealth.

🌐 🌐 🌐

As one other example, I'd like to take you through much of what I do on an ongoing basis to promote myself, make myself viable, support myself as a valuable brand, and fuel the businesses that support me. I realize, of course, you are most likely in a very dif-ferent business than mine so many of the specifics may not apply. More do than you might first think, though. But it's more impor-tant to grasp the magnitude of the whirling dervish housed here at the Dan Kennedy Command Center, and to grasp the all-important idea of having many, many, many, many doors open and welcoming in new customers. One welcome mat for wealth won't do. So, my list, not necessarily in any priority order:

- **Books.** Obviously, I write books, and then promote my books, and have my books and new book launches as excuse for promoting me. There's a list of all of them now in print on page 243. Each year I have at least one new or revised, updated but recycled one released, and in most years, more than one. There are books getting started, books being written, books getting finished and shipped off to publishers, book promotions beginning, in progress, and ending, virtually every day, continuously. We have had as many as 15,000 people attend "a teleseminar with the author" connected to my books, thanks to getting hundreds of other authors, advisors to industries, associations, our own Members, business owners of every stripe, and my personal friends to promote it. I have done a four-cities-in-four-days book tour by private jet, personally speaking to over 1,200 people and generating buzz, done in-store book signings attended by as many as 300, blitzes of radio interviews, and lobbied for and gotten "ink" (exposure and praise) in magazines and newspapers, including *USA Today* and *Inc.* and *Entrepreneur* magazines. Much of this is just not possible without the books. It's my contention, incidentally, that every businessperson should write a book and have it as a promotional tool.

- **Radio and Teleseminar Interviews**. Most weeks, two or three, sometimes more. Some connected to my role as political commentary columnist with BusinessAnd Media.org, more connected to my books, or to Glazer-Kennedy Insider's Circle™. The teleseminars are usually put on by other leaders of industries, industry groups, or associations, and I'm there as guest expert.

- **"Fan Mail."** I get a lot of correspondence from Glazer-Kennedy Insider's Circle™ Members, readers of my books, people who hear me speak, and so forth. Some ask questions, some tell me of their successes. I read it all, answer much of it personally, delegate some, answer some in newsletters or online. Some weeks, maybe only a couple dozen. Other weeks, that number multiplied. In a year, thousands. About half of this is with Members, so you might categorize it as "customer service," although that would be underestimating its significance. The other half is with people who are not yet Members but may join, or who've bought and read one book who may buy them all, who have no relationship but may develop one—even leading to a good consulting engagement for me. The daily and weekly flow of correspondence crossing my desk that must be responded to is daunting—but any one piece might be the piece connected to the person who, sooner or later, is worth $10,000.00 or $100,000.00 or $1-million to me.

- **Thank-You Notes, Congratulation Notes**. People send me copies of articles they think I'll find interesting or can use in my newsletters, send me photos, gifts. They all get thanked. Anytime somebody refers somebody to me or otherwise assists me, they get thanked. If I read about one of our Members, another author or speaker I know, another contact in a publication, or I see them on TV, or hear them on the radio, or am told they were there by somebody else, I drop them a congratulatory note. This reminds people I'm around, reminds them they might have reason to conduct some business with us or tell somebody about us.

- **Articles.** I pump out a lot of articles for others to use, that keep me living in their newsletters, magazines, blogs, and other media. We formally syndicate some articles from Glazer-Kennedy Insider's Circle™ I personally write some for different outlets, I encourage reprinting excerpts from my books. I look for people who have the same kind of customers as we do or clients as I do, with whom I am not directly competitive, and actively work at being shown to their customers by them, as often as possible.

- **Speaking**. Way back when, early in my business life, promoting on a local level, I spoke just about anywhere good customers for me might be found, free for a year or so, then for fees as well as promotion. The first year, I spoke at more than 100 in-office sales meetings of different small companies alone, plus other venues. Heck, if you had a birthday party of any size, you could skip the clown; I'd come speak. For a decade, nationally, I spoke professionally, and was very well compensated, some 60 to 75 times a year and just about lived at airports and hotels, acquiring lots of customers with lasting value every step of the way. Today, I speak much more sparingly and selectively, about three to five times a year outside of Glazer-Kennedy Insider's Circle.™ Each such engagement involves a lot of advance promotion, preparation, and after-the-fact follow up to harvest all the benefits.

- **Other "Pressing of the Flesh."** My private clients often rise up out of large numbers of people who attend Glazer-Kennedy Insider's Circle™ conferences, or come to local Chapter meetings, or know of me from many things but finally get to have a face-to-face conversation with me at some event. Several times a year I put myself in such an environment. For many years, I did so much more often. I also find that "manufactured social settings" are very valuable. In my case, that means hosting things like a Night at the Races after a multi-day seminar I've spoken at, giving me an opportunity to just hang out with people. This usually yields business on the spot or immediately afterward.

- **Connecting.** I've organized things so I'm at the center of big circles of people and businesses and things going on around me, and made a point of building one helluva a Rolodex.® If I don't personally know the person you need or the person who should be linked with you to produce big profits from married opportunities and assets, I at least know the person who *does* know that person. I do a fair amount of behind-the-scenes, uncompensated brokering of relationships, deals, match-ups that benefit both. This builds up the bank of goodwill I can call on as needed or as opportunities present themselves.

- **Deal-Making.** I'm often putting one of the businesses I am connected to together with an outside company, so we can leverage something they have, and they can profit from something we have.

- **Regular Writing Workload.** I write five newsletters, a weekly fax, periodically post to a blog, and several new multi-media home study courses or online courses or multi-day seminars per year, for Glazer-Kennedy Insider's Circle.™ This is product we deliver but it is also ongoing promotion, interesting people in what's new, keeping people interested in us. It's the glue of the entire multi-million dollar, diversified, and far-flung enterprise. I also write sales letters and marketing materials.

In addition to all this, I maintain a busy schedule of private consulting days, major advertising copywriting work as a freelancer for clients, a day each month of back-to-back private coaching calls with my Platinum clients, several multi-day meetings a year for them, a group call once a month for Diamond-level Glazer-Kennedy Insider's Circle™ Members, an extensive research and information gathering effort, occasional travel to meetings or speaking engagements, and, of course, the nitty-gritty grunt work of running my little business, which I do with but one staff-person, located far away. (The Glazer-Kennedy Insider's Circle™ business is run by Bill Glazer with some 30 employees.)

Every day, a multitude of things to keep the pipeline primed with new business, and to respond to the business reaching boiling point, and to deliver the work already committed, are all going on simultaneously at quick pace, and typically under deadline pressure.

I'm confident, if you were to shadow me for a week, you'd leave saying it's no wonder he's so successful—look at *everything* he does. I've dealt with the "how can he do all this?" in my book *No B.S. Time Management for Entrepreneurs*, if I aroused curiosity about that.

So here it is. Those who seem to easily attract more opportunity, more co-operation, more resources, more success, more recognition, and more wealth than any one person could ever need or want may do it easily, but not effortlessly. In fact, they do it by creating a powerful magnetic force manufactured, essentially, by running around in a circle managing a multitude of activities around that circle, at very, very high speed and frenetic pace. The resulting energy is very attractive.

WEALTH RESOURCES

Recommended Books and Reading,
Websites, Contacts, and Free Offer
from the Author

Bank of
Wealth Resources

Free Audio Programs Online

www.NoBSBooks.com

WEALTH ATTRACTION: Live-recorded highlights from my Wealth Attraction Seminar and my Renegade Millionaire System

TAKING ACTION: Live-recorded interview with Robert Ringer, author of the *New York Times* bestseller *Winning Through Intimidation,* the revised version, *To Be or Not To Be Intimidated,* and *Action: Nothing Happens Until Something Moves*

Free Video Programs Online

www.NoBSBooks.com

DAN KENNEDY INTERVIEWS with Kristi Frank, from Donald Trump's *The Apprentice*

NO B.S. BUSINESS SUCCESS FOR THE NEW ECONOMY–live recorded Q/A

NO B.S. SALES SUCCESS FOR THE NEW ECONOMY–live recorded Q/A

Free Webinars/Free Membership

Return the Acceptance Form on page 251 and you'll be provided access to the series of three Glazer-Kennedy University Webinars as well as a free trial Glazer-Kennedy Insider's Circle™ Membership.

People from this Book I Recommend Reading About, Studying, Getting to Know

Buffett, Warren. Investor. I recommend reading the biography *Snowball* (by Alice Schroeder), *Warren Buffett Speaks* (by Janet Lowe), and *Thoughts of Chairman Buffett* (by Simon Reynolds).

Cossman, E. Joseph. Mail-order entrepreneur. Popularized The Ant Farm. Read: *How To Make at Least One Million Dollars in Mail–Order* by Cossman.

Dennis, Felix. Publishing industry entrepreneur best known for creating *Maxim* magazine. Author of *How To Get Rich*.

Furey, Matt. Author of *Combat Conditioning*. Health and fitness guru and promoter in the grand tradition of Charles Atlas. Matt is also the current keeper of the Maxwell Maltz/*Psycho-Cybernetics* legacy and all related intellectual properties, and an expert teacher of success philosophy. MattFurey.com

Hansen, Mark Victor. Author, speaker, entrepreneur. Best-known as co-creator of the *Chicken Soup for the Soul* book series.

His most recent book *Richest Kids in America* profiles extraordinary child-entrepreneurs.

Hibbard, Foster. Metaphysical author and lecturer, famous for his Millionaire's Seminar. In the latter years of his career, Foster was a close associate of mine, we developed over a dozen audio programs, and he conducted over 300 seminars for my companies. Referenced here with regard to his powerful Wealth Account/ Giving Account concept. I am currently working on re-editing, re-mastering, and producing a new collection of Foster Hibbard recordings. You may contact me directly via fax at (602) 269–3113 for information.

Hill, Napoleon. At Andrew Carnegie's behest, conducted extensive research, from 1917 to 1935, into the most successful inventors, industrialists, entrepreneurs, and others, then published his findings in several books, most notably the legendary *Think and Grow Rich*. www.NapoleonHillFoundation.com

Houdini. Yes, *that* Houdini. Referenced in this book re. the Wealth Magnet of Demonstration. I highly, highly, highly recommend reading the best biography of him, *The Secret Life of Houdini* (by Kalush and Sloman). Additional information can be found at www.apl.org/history/houdini/biography.com and www.magic tricks.com/houdini.

Kragen, Ken. Professional publicist, known for launching careers of numerous celebrities. Author, *Life Is a Contact Sport*.

Kramer, Dr. Edward. Author, early leader in self-improvement and success philosophy, proponent of controversial theories including The Sidis Method and Synchromatics. Inventor of the '"Thank-U-Gram," a very popular product in its time, featured in *Reader's Digest* and used and praised by numerous celebrities including Bob Hope and Dr. Norman Vincent Peale. To the best of my knowledge, Dr. Kramer's works are all out of print but worth searching for.

Maltz, Dr. Maxwell. Developed and popularized the concept of self-image psychology. His book *Psycho-Cybernetics*, originally published in 1960, was a major bestseller and has continued its life through word-of-mouth for 40+ years, selling, in all editions, an estimated 30-million copies. I co-authored an updated version of the book, *The New Psycho-Cybernetics*, as well as an audio program *The New Psycho-Cybernetics* published by the Nightingale-Conant Corporation. Current information about other Psycho-Cybernetics resources can be found via MattFurey.com.

Newman, Paul. Actor, race-car driver, entrepreneur, political activist, and philanthropist. I recommend reading the biography *Paul Newman: A Life* (by Shawn Levy) and the book describing his entrepreneurial exploits with Newman's Own foods, *Shameless Exploitation* (by Paul Newman and A.E.Hotchner).

Nightingale, Earl. Radio broadcaster who, inspired by *Think and Grow Rich,* became an author and, for many years, the leading voice of success philosophy in America. His recording, *The Strangest Secret,* is the all-time bestselling spoken-word recording in this genre, and the only one ever to be recognized with a Gold Record-putting Earl right up there with Elvis and Sinatra. www.Nightingale-Conant.com, and www.DianaNightingale.com. Earl provided one of the fundamental tenets of my Renegade Millionaire System. www.RenegadeMillionaire.com

Ogilvy, David. One of the pioneers of modern advertising, who built from scratch one of the largest advertising agencies of his time. Ogilvy transcended creating advertising to developing and teaching a definitive philosophy about it. The latest biography, *The King of Madison Avenue* (by Kenneth Roman) is essential reading. If you have or develop a strong interest in advertising, get *Ogilvy On Advertising* as well.

Qubein, Nido R. Author, speaker, consultant; Chairman, Great Harvest Bread Company; President, High Point University.

HighPoint.edu. NidoQubein.com. Nido has appeared at Glazer-Kennedy Insider's Circle™ SuperConferences as one of the speakers in our CEO Series, which has also featured Jim McCann (1-800-Flowers) and Terry Jones (Travelocity). SPECIAL NOTE: I am working with Nido on a new career/business training program for executives and entrepreneurs transitioning to authorship, consulting, business coaching, and speaking, presented in association with High Point University. If interested, contact me personally by fax: (602) 269–3113.

Ramsey, David. Personal finance expert, radio/TV talk show host. A voice of reason and common sense with regard to debt. DaveRamsey.com

Ringer, Robert. Author, classic bestseller, *Winning Through Intimidation*. www.RobertRinger.com. To hear my interview with Robert Ringer, visit www.NoBSBooks.com.

Rohn, Jim. One of the most influential contemporary voices of success philosophy. Hundreds of thousands have attended his lectures, seminars, and retreats. JimRohn.com

Ross, George. The chief negotiator for the Trump Organization and Donald Trump's righthand man since the start of Trump's empire-building. Author, *Trump Strategies for Real Estate: Billionaire Lessons for the Small Investor*. I recommend reading it whether you are a real estate investor or not.

Simmons, Gene. Created rock band KISS. Author, *Sex, Money, KISS*. Gene is one of the many fascinating celebrity-entrepreneurs who have appeared at Glazer-Kennedy Insider's Circle™ SuperConferences. www.GeneSimmons.com

Trump, Donald. Needs no description unless you are an alien just arrived from another planet. Author of a number of books–I recommend you read them all.

Turner, Glenn W. Founder and super-promoter of a group of direct sales/multilevel marketing companies in the 1970s that enjoyed meteoric growth and then was attacked by government regulators. Glenn became one of the most controversial figures of his time. Created the self-improvement program *Dare To Be Great*. www.GlennTurner.com

Vance, Mike. Former Dean of Disney University. Close associate of Walt's during development of Disney World and planning of Epcot. Creativity and innovation advisor to many leading corporations. Author, *Think Outside the Box* and *Raising the Bar*.

Ziglar, Zig. Author, one of the top bestselling self-improvement books of all time, *See You at the Top*. My speaking colleague of nine consecutive years on the number-one seminar tour in America, the star-studded SUCCESS events drawing from 10,000 to 35,000 in 25 to 27 cities a year. ZigZiglar.com

Planet Dan Folks Mentioned in this Book

Coutu, Diana. Diana's Gourmet Pizzeria in Winnipeg, Canada. Amazing entrepreneur, promoter, author, international chef competition winner and judge, seen on The Food Network. Visit: www.OneGreatPizza.ca and www.DianasGourmetPizzeria.ca.

Garman, Darin. Heartland-of-America real estate investing expert. Works directly with thousands of investors. Heartland InvestmentBook.com

Garratt, Owen. Famous pencil artist. www.pencilneck.com

Glazer, Bill. Author of *Outrageous Advertising That's Outrageously Successful*. Has provided advertising training and campaigns to more than 10,000 independent retailers, evolved from his own exceptional success as owner of retail stores. President of Glazer-Kennedy Insider's Circle™ the leading association of marketing-oriented entrepreneurs, business owners, and professionals, with more than 25,000 active Members worldwide, over 250,000 online subscribers and customers, and media, including three newsletters that reach millions. Bill is an expert teacher of advertising, marketing, and sales strategies—and you can meet him via the free Glazer-Kennedy University Webinars provided to you when you return the Acceptance Form on page 251.

Gravette, Michael, CEO, SafetyTechnology.com, and Safe FamilyLife.com. Developer of internet marketing-driven businesses, online catalogs, direct-selling organizations, distributor networks and retail distribution, presently for personal, family, home, and small business security products.

Guthy, Bill and Greg Renker. Founders, Guthy-Renker Corporation, the leading television infomercial company featuring countless celebrities in its programs. Extremely adept at creating and establishing leading brands in skin care, cosmetics, nutrition, and health via television infomercials, then expanding each by multi-channel marketing and distribution. They built their billion-dollar entity from zero. Guthy-Renker.com

Hammond, Bill. Attorney, author, and business/marketing coach to elder law attorneys nationwide. www.kcelderlaw.com

Hurn, Chris. CEO, Mercantile Capital, nationwide commercial lender to small business owners with emphasis on owner-occupied real estate. CEO, Kennedy's All-American Barber Club, nationwide franchise network of upscale men's barber shops. You can communicate with Chris directly at churn@mercantilecc.com.

Killingbeck, Dean. CEO, Get Customers Now—the leading provider of completely done for clients, targeted direct-mail campaigns for local businesses of all kinds, including innovative, high-yield birthday, anniversary, and new-mover campaigns. GetCustomersNowMarketing.com

LeGrand, Ron. Author of *Quick–Turn Real Estate*. Leader of the independent, entrepreneurial real estate investing movement in America. RonLeGrand.com

Lycka, Dr. Barry. Operates a large, thriving cosmetic practice as well as a day spa in Canada. Business consultant and advisor to others in his profession. www.barrylyckamd.com

Tomshack, Dr. Chris. CEO, HealthSource, a nationwide network of franchised chiropractic and weight loss clinics. www.Health Source.com

Tubbergen, Dennis. CEO, provides marketing and business training, celebrity–endorsed marketing programs, proprietary financial products and a full range of support services for independent financial advisors. Also publishes financial and wealth information for affluent entrepreneurs and investors. www.Dennis Tubbergen.com

Other Planet Dan Experts and Entrepreneurs You May Find Helpful

Altadonna, Dr. Ben. Leading advisor on practice marketing to the chiropractic profession. Altadonna Communications. Fax (925) 314–9442.

Cardell, Chris. Brilliant expert in internet marketing, for all kinds of businesses; small or large; retail or service; consumer or B2B; local or global. www.CardellMedia.com

Galper, Ari. Creator of the ChatWise® system for instant, "live" discussion with website visitors to dramatically improve conversion and sales results, and of Unlock The Game®, a revolutionary approach to stress-free selling. www.Chatwise.com

Geier, Jay. Scheduling Institute of America. Provides training and sophisticated system to improve front desk staff's successful management of in-bound calls from prospective patients, clients, or customers, predominately in professional practices. www.SchedulingInstitute.com

Harrison, Bill and Stephen. Publicity experts, publishers of *Book Marketing Up–Date* (for authors) and *Radio/TV Interview Report* (for the media), hosts of The National Publicity Summit (where authors and entrepreneurs meet media contacts in a "speed–dating" format), and consultants/coaches to entrepreneurs on Make-Your-Business-Famous strategies. www.Rtir.com

Ipach, Ron. Top marketing and business advisor to the auto repair industry. Also a coach to owners of all kinds of businesses on accelerated and easier implementation through effective use of freelancers, online resources, outsourcing. www.Cinron.com

Kern, Frank. Author, *The Mass Control System*. Dangerous genius (!) at psychology-driven sales and marketing with online media. www.Superbadkern.com

Lillo, Pete. Known far and wide as "Pete the Printer," Pete provides print-marketing advice and specialty direct-mail campaign turn-key production and execution, Done4You® customer newsletters, and other services, as well as publishing my newsletter expressly for direct–response copywriters and marketers, *Look Over My Shoulder*, and licensing co-author/reprint rights to a number of my publications, including the book *Ultimate Success Secret*. www.PeteThePrinter.com

Milteer, Lee. With Bill Glazer at Glazer-Kennedy Insider's Circle,™ Lee leads our Peak Performers Group, a business coaching and international mastermind group meeting several times a year and working together otherwise via teleconferencing and online. Lee is a celebrated peak performance coach, with prestigious corporate clients that have included Federal Express and the Walt Disney Company. She is the author of two books, *Success Is an Inside Job* and *Spiritual Selling Tools*. Her Millionaire Smarts interviews and audio programs are incorporated into many niche-industry advisors', publishers', and associations' programs for their members, in total reaching more than 100,000 listeners per month. www.LeeMilteer.com

O'Keefe, Ed, CEO, Dentist Profits, Inc. Consultant/coach to the dental profession, specializing in "The $100,000.00 Day In Any Office" and comprehensive marketing for specialized treatments or services, such as implant dentistry or sedation dentistry. www.DentistProfits.com

Oliver, Stephen. NAPMA—National Association of Professional Martial Artists, the trade associations of martial arts school owners and instructors. Also, a franchisor of martial arts academies. www.NAPMA.com. www.MileHighKarate.com

Orent, Dr. Tom. Practice development, business, and wealth coach to dentists. Publishes the #1 practice-building newsletter in dentistry. www.1000Gems.com

Organizations Referenced in this Book

Business And Media Institute, a watchdog group, think-tank, and advocacy group focused on liberal media bias in reporting on business and political issues. BMI monitors the news media, prepares and issues extensively researched Special Reports, publishes and syndicates articles and columns, and provides expert guests to radio and television programs on a regular basis. They are aggressive champions of free enterprise. I'm proud to be associated with BMI, and to have my political opinion columns published regularly at www.BusinessAndMedia.org.

Glazer–Kennedy Insider's Circle™, a "place" for entrepreneurs, business owners, sales professionals and self-employed professionals with strong interest in marketing and enthusiasm for creative innovation to network and share information online, at international conferences, and at the local level, with local Chapters and Kennedy Study/Mastermind Groups. A directory of local Chapters and other information can be accessed at www. DanKennedy.com.

Information Marketing Association (IMA) is the trade association and membership organization for authors and thought-leaders, business advisors and coaches, speakers and seminar leaders, newsletter publishers, and internet marketers. IMA offers online training and other resources for beginners and novices as well as for established, experienced info-marketers, as well as a full range of support and services, from professional liability insurance to publishing assistance. www.info-marketing.org.

High Point University is an exciting, progressive university specializing in business, finance, and communications. www.High Point.edu

About the Author

D AN KENNEDY is a multi-millionaire serial entrepreneur, sought-after marketing consultant, and strategic advisor, speaker, author with a 30-year track record of helping entrepreneurs attract and create wealth in a diverse variety of product, service, business, industry, and professional categories. He lives, most of the time, in northeastern Ohio, where he owns and races harness horses, and drives professionally himself in more than 150 races a year. His office is in Phoenix, Arizona, and should you wish to contact him directly about speaking, consulting, or just your comments about this book, you are welcome to do so by fax at (602) 269-3113. (He does not use e-mail; please do not send e-mail for him to any of the websites with which he is associated, listed in this book.) Inquiries concerning

Glazer-Kennedy Insider's Circle™ membership, programs, and services should be directed to www.DanKennedy.com.

Other Books by the Author

The No B.S. Series (Entrepreneur Press)

No B.S. Business Success for The New Economy

No B.S. Direct Marketing for Non-Direct Marketing Businesses

No B.S. Marketing to The Affluent

No B.S. Ruthless Management of People and Profits

No B.S. Sales Success for The New Economy

No B.S. Time Management for Entrepreneurs

Make Millions With Your Ideas (Penguin/Plume)

My Unfinished Business: Autobiographical Essays (Glazer-Kennedy Insider's Circle™)

The New Psycho-Cybernetics with Dr. Maxwell Maltz (Prentice-Hall)

The Official Get Rich Guide to Information Marketing with Bill Glazer, Robert Skrob, and the Information Marketing Association (Entrepreneur Press)

Ultimate Marketing Plan (Adams Media)

Ultimate Sales Letter (Adams Media)

Uncensored Sales Strategies with Sydney Barrows (Entrepreneur Press)

Zero Resistance Selling (Prentice-Hall)

Index

A

abundance, belief in, 15
action, taking, 82, 84, 87, 91
Action! Nothing Happens Until Something Moves, 83, 84
affluency/affluent lifestyle, 16, 19, 22–23, 73–74
Aldrin, Buzz, 200
Allen, Paul, 190
Allen, Robert, 167
Allen, Woody, 50
Allen Brothers, 129
alliances, strategic, 119
Altadonna, Dr. Ben, 238
Always Bear Left, 172
Amazing Kreskin, 189
Amazon, 190, 192
ambition vs. greed, 35
American Greetings Corporation, 38
America's Best Colleges (*U.S. News and World Report*), 199
amusement park industry, 19

Amway, 129
The Ant Farm, 88
The Apprentice, 54, 67, 97, 161, 178, 185
Ask magnet, 117–120
assets, developing and owning, 112
attitude about wealth, 22
authenticity, 100, 116
autonomy, 149
Avon, 63, 129

B

Banking, Present and Future, 156–158
bankruptcies, 41, 43
author's experience and recovery, 44–45
barbershop franchise example, 207–218
Barnum, P.T., 42
The Baron, 133–134
behavioral congruency, 163–166, 173
being somewhere for opportunity, 77–78
Bergdorf Goodman, 17

Be Somebody magnet, 69, 211
Be Somewhere magnet, 76, 212
Bezos, 190, 192
blaming, 54
Blockbuster, 139
Book Marketing Up-Date, 239
boundaries, 136, 138–140
Branson, Richard, 105
Buffett, Warren, 101, 128, 232
Buick, David, 42
Burnett, Mark, 161
Bush, President, 69
business(es)
excuses for not doing well in, 49
fear-based, 43
market-driven, 124, 125
second, 208
Business and Media Institute, 21–22, 240

C

Caesars Palace, 184
Camp, Jim, 165

Canada's Best Pizzas Cookbook, 221
Canfield, Jack, 57–58
Cardell, Chris, 238
Carter, Jimmy, 147
Celebrity Apprentice, 67, 78, 185
celebrity marketing, 69, 70, 71–72
CEO
 greed, 150–151
 pay, high, 48–49, 52
Cerebrus, 131
ChatWise®, 238
Chicken Soup for the Soul, 58, 118, 167, 233
"chore to more," 207–208
clarity, 141–143
Clason, George, 170
Clinton, President Bill, 200
closing the sale, 8–9
coaching groups, 18–19, 64–65, 114–115, 132, 239
 Harrison, Bill and Stephen, 239
 Hurn, Harter and Worrall, 209
Coca–Cola, 103
Combat Conditioning, 137, 232
Combined Insurance Companies of America, 190
commerce, 39
commodity, 133
confidence, 45, 60, 147
congruent behavior, 163–166, 173
The Consumers' Guide to Cosmetic Surgery, 71
Cosby, Bill, 70, 200
Cossman, Joe, 88, 129, 232
Coutu, Diana, 62, 72
Coutu, Pierre, 62
courage, 181–183
courtesy, 152
Crawford, Cindy, 130
creative vision, 47
Chrysler, 82, 131
Culp, Robert, 102

D
Dare To Be Great (Turner), 236
deadlines, meeting, 115, 164
deal-making, 185–188, 227
debt, 147–149
demands, unreasonable, 154
Demonstration, 94–102
Dennis, Felix, 126, 232
Diana's Gourmet Pizzeria, 71, 72, 220–222, 236
Dillinger, John, 31
direct marketing, 89, 132
discipline, self-, 52, 91–92
Disney/WaltDisney/ Disney World, 42, 101, 103, 104–106, 112–113, 184–185, 190, 192, 196, 236
distribution of successful product, 63–64
The DNA of Success, 93
domino opportunity, 120–121
Don't Squat With Yer Spurs On, 80
Do Something magnet, 81, 214
Dr. 90210, 71
Dr. Phil, 69, 120

E
"easy money," 61
Edison, Thomas, 94–95
Eli Bridge Company, 19
emotional resiliency, 42
energy
 from people, 175–177
 kinetic, 187
E network, 71, 105
engineering situations, 33
entitlement notion, 33, 153
entrepreneur(s)
 child, 233
 courageous, 182
 income priority of, 155
 millionaires, 169, 172
 process approach, 108
 "rags to riches," 81
 responsibility, 37
 successful, 34, 40, 42, 51

 teaching to be, 61
 super-wealthy, 159, 166, 201, 219
equity, not income, 155–156
excuse-making, 49, 50, 54–56
experience, 190
expertise, not location, 139
expert status, 72–75, 79, 182, 211

F
"fair share"/"fairness," fallacy, 4, 27, 28, 29, 31, 32, 33
fear
 about money, 43–44, 60
 rule of, 46
Fiji Water, 111
financial
 advisors, 62, 183
 success, 27
fire alarm business, example, 39
Floor Coverings International, 110
Folger, James, 42
follow-up, 108, 111, 112–113
Forbes, Steve, 200
Forbes 400 list of richest people, 51
Forbes magazine
 advertising in, 137
 celebrity listing, 70
Ford company, 82
Ford, Henry, 42
Ford, President (Gerald), 69
Foreman, George, 69
Forum Shops (Las Vegas), 17
Fox, William, 42
franchising/franchises, 61–62, 87, 208, 217
Furey, Matt, 137–138, 232
Future Banking, 156–158

G
Garman, Darin, 70–71, 74, 137, 179, 236

Garrett, Owen, 62–63, 236
gas station/convenience
     store, 64
Gates, Bill, 190, 192
Geier, Jay, 238
Gentlemen's Domain cata-
     log, 19
geographic limitations, 139
Get Customers Now, 156,
     237
The Girls Next Door, 105
Giving Account, 170–171
Glazer, Bill, 89–90, 131–132,
     179
Glazer–Kennedy Insider's
     Circle™, 54, 67, 72, 77,
     83, 89, 90, 121, 129, 130,
     156, 179, 192, 195, 224,
     225, 226, 227, 232,
     236–237, 239, 240–241
Glazer–Kennedy University
     Webinars, 232
goals, behavioral, 165
Gold Star Syndrome, 109–110
Gravette, Michael, 222–223,
     237
Great Depression, 43, 46–47
Great Harvest Bread
     Company, 195, 234
greed, 34, 35, 150–151
Greenspan, Alan, 47
Greenwood, Lee, 200
Giuliani, Rudy, 200
Guthy, Bill, 63, 237
Guthy-Renker Corporation,
     63, 70, 88, 95, 129

H
Habitforce, 171–172, 173–174
Halbert, Gary, 52, 80, 81,
     89, 220
Hammond, Bill, 74, 237
Hansen, Mark Victor, 113,
     167, 233
"hard-earned dollars," 60
Harley-Davidson sales
     focus, 78
Harrison, Bill and Stephen,
     239
Hathaway shirts, 133–135

HealthSource, 61, 238
Hefner, Hugh, 98–99, 100,
     102–107
Heinz, H.J., 42
Hibbard, Foster, 171, 172,
     232–233
"hidden money," 20–21
High Point University
     (HPU), 195–205, 235, 241
Hill, Napoleon, 43, 57, 59,
     171–172, 233
Hilton, Conrad, 42
Home Depot, 130–131
home-shopping channels
     (HSN, QVC), 86–87, 97
Houdini, 95, 233
How To Get Rich, 126, 232
*How To Make at Least One
     Million Dollars in Mail-
     Order*, 232
*How To Make Millions with
     Your Ideas*, 86
Hurn, Chris, 207–218, 237

I
Iacocca, Lee, 82, 178
Imbev/Anheuser–Busch,
     190–191
inaction, reasons for, 86
income, vs, equity, 155–158
independence, 116–117,
     146–147
infomercials, TV, 70, 86, 129,
     184
Information Marketing
     Association (IMA), 90,
     241
*Insider Secrets To Delivering
     Red Carpet Service: The
     Celebrity Experience*,
     196–197
integrity, 37–38, 116, 153,
     214–215
intelligence, innate, 189–190
International Hardware
     Retailers Association
     example, 109
internet marketing, 135,
     136–139, 238
Investors Business Daily, 137

Ipach, Ron, 239

J
Jackson, Michael, 98
James, Jessie, 31
J.C. Penney, 42
Jesus Christ, teaching
     about fear, 43
Jones, Jim, 235
Johnson, Chelsea, 205
Johnson, Dr. Michael,
     25–26
Judith Z., 152–153

K
Karrass, Charles, 28, 29
Kennedy, Dan
     bankruptcy, 44–45
     bio, 242–243
     books, 243
     chiropractic profession,
          marketing to,
          127–128
     Coaching Groups,
          18–19, 64–65, 114–115
     compensation/fees,
          51–52
     demonstration, 98–100
     direct marketing, 72, 73
     mastermind groups,
          179, 240
     Platinum Mastermind
          Group, 209
     promotion, 223–228
     publications, 16, 48, 86,
          218
     racehorse involvement,
          75, 86, 99, 185
     speaking history, 225–226
     websites, 17, 72, 79
Kennedy's All–American
     Barber Club®, 207–218,
     237
Kern, Frank, 239
Killingbeck, Dean, 156–157,
     237
Kincade, Thomas, 28
Kindle®, 139
kinetic energy, 187
King, Larry, 70

King, Stephen, 28
The King of Madison Avenue,
    96, 234
KISS rock band, 12, 182, 235
Kotler, Dr. Robert, 71
Kragen, Ken, 121, 233
Kramer, Dr. Edward, 170,
    189, 191, 233

L
Laws of Success, 43, 172
lawyers
    coaching, 114–115
    trade journal, 121
La–Z–Boy, 195
LeGrand, Ron, 65, 237
Life Is a Contact Sport, 233
Lillo, Pete, 179, 239
limited wealth belief, 5–7
Little Black Book, 102
Look Over My Shoulder, 239
losers, 55
Lycka, Dr. Barry, 70, 238

M
Madoff, Bernie, 31
Make-Your-Business-
    Famous strategies, 239
Maltz, Maxwell, 91, 173,
    232, 234
market
    demand, 124
    hidden money in, 20–21
    share, 4
    timing, 190–191
marketing
    direct–mail, restaurant
        example, 156–157
    Kennedy's All-
        American Barber
        Club®, 207
    lessons in, 103–104
    plans, 141
    strategist, 52
marketing prowess mag-
    net, 159–162, 217
marketplace
    celebrity-driven, 69
    changing, 82
    niche, 90
    respect, 152

Mary Kay, 63, 129
The Mass Control System, 239
maturity, 124
MAXIM magazine, 126,
    232
Mays, Billy, 64
McCann, Jim, 69, 235
McGraw, Phil, 120
McMahon, Vince, 105
media environment,
    95–96, 122
Mercantile Capital
    Corporation, 209, 218
metaphysical view of
    prosperity and money,
    27, 30, 123, 125
Meyer, Paul J., 143
Microsoft, 190
millionaires
    entrepreneurial, 169
    "from-scratch," 83–84,
        163–164, 172
    prevalence of, 23
Millionaire magazine, 17
The Millionaire Next Door, 169
Milteer, Lee, 56, 179, 239–240
mind, conditioning, 18
modeling, 164
mommy-blogging, 23–24
money
    fears/anxiety about,
        43–44, 60, 144
    movement of, 182
    nature of, 30–31
    replaceable, 45
    speaking about, 59–60
Montessori, 189
Moore, Michael, 22

N
Nardelli, Bob, 130–131
National Association of
    Professional Martial
    Artists, 240
National Publicity
    Summit, 239
negotiation, 28
Neiman-Marcus catalogs,
    19, 20
Nemeth, Maria, 30

NetJets, 16, 101, 103, 128
Newman, Jim, 24
Newman, Paul, and
    Newman's Own brand,
    13–14, 234
The New Psycho-Cybernetics,
    173, 234, 243
newsmongering, 21–22
Nightingale, Earl, 43,
    72–73, 220, 234
90-Day Experiment,
    168–171
9/11 attack, as example of
    fault–finding, 29–30
No B.S. Books series and
    website, 79, 119, 144,
    231–232, 235, 243
    Business Success, 48
    *DIRECT Marketing for
        NON–Direct
        Marketing Businesses*,
        132, 161
    Marketing Letter, 161,
        179, 191–192
    *Marketing to the
        Affluent*, 129, 206
    *Ruthless Management of
        People and Profits*,
        143, 180
    *Sales Success for The New
        Economy*, 83, 161
    *Time Management for
        Entrepreneurs*, 99,
        143, 180, 228
No Guilt magnet, 3–11,
    209–210

O
observation, acute, 189
Ogilvy, David, 52, 96, 97,
    133–135, 234
Ogilvy on Advertising, 234
O'Keefe, Ed, 240
Oliver, Stephen, 240
Omaha Steaks, 129
One Minute Millionaire, 167
opportunism, 38–40, 47
opportunity, 51, 61, 77–78,
    82, 89, 108, 197, 206
    domino, 120–122

exposure to, 132
independence and, 146
wasted, 110
optimism, reasoned, 47
Orent, Dr. Tom, 240
Outrageous Advertising That's Outrageously Successful, 90, 236

P

pace, 184–185, 187–189
Palin, Sarah, 97–98
passion for wealth, 123, 125–126
Passionate About Pizza, 221
Patterson, James, 28
Paul Newman: A Life, 234
Pennsylvania Lawyer, 121
people, negative versus positive, 176–177
Pink Panther movies, 55
Pitney-Bowes, 109
place strategy, 79–80
"Planet Dan," 180
Playboy, 98, 102–107
POM Wonderful Nutrition Company, 111
Popeil, Ron, 64
Powell, General Colin, 69
power
    derived from responsibility, 48, 56, 60
    drainers, 178
"power team," 178–180
pragmatism, 114, 116
Present Banking, 156–158
pressure-prosperity link, 54–55
price(s)
    competition, 115
    elasticity, 8
    premium, 74
Principal, Victoria, 63, 129–130
Pro-Activ, 63–64, 130
process approach, 108, 111–112
profits, 35–39, 74, 143
promises not kept, 115, 116

prosperity
    metaphysical view, 27
    spiritual beliefs, 189
prudent behavior, 47
Psycho-Cybernetics Foundation, 138
Psycho-Cybernetics, 91, 173, 232, 234
publicity, celebrity, 71
punctuality, 115

Q

Qubein, Dr. Nido R., 195–201, 203, 205, 234–235
Quick-Turn Real Estate, 237

R

Radio/TV Interview Report, 239
Raising the Bar, 236
Ramsey, Dave, 147, 235
Rancic, Bill, 54–55
Randi, Dr. James, 95
rarity, 112–113
rational thought, 47
Reagan, President, 69
recession
    media hype about, 21–22, 47
    post-, 46–47, 79, 81, 135
    trust during, 74
Release Your Brakes, 24
reliability, 116
Renegade Millionaire System, 102–107, 130, 131, 149, 156, 163, 187, 234
Renker, Greg, 63, 88, 89, 237
reputation, 52–53
resiliency, emotional, 42
Resnick, Lynda, 111
respect
    personal, 54, 116, 152
    for wealth, 144
responsibility
author's 53–54
    differential, CEO, 49
    entrepreuneurial, 21, 35–37, 39–40
    risks and success, 48, 50–51, 57–58

transfer of, 183
rich, demonization of, 51
Richest Kids in America, 233
Richest Man in Babylon, 170
Ringer, Robert, 83, 84, 235
risk-taking, 42, 51, 181
Rivers, Joan, 69, 78, 93
Robbins, Tony, 95
The Robb Report, 17, 19
Rodeo Drive (Beverly Hills), 17
Rogers, Kenny, 121, 144
Rohn, Jim, 26, 32, 219–220, 235
Rolls-Royce example, 96
Ross, George, 97, 178, 235
Ryan, Pat, 104

S

SafeTechnologies/SafeFamilyLife/SafeLife Kits, 222–223, 237
Sally R., 25–26
saving, 169–170
Scarborough, Donald, 196, 198–205
Scheduling Institute of America, 238
Schwartzkopf, General Norman, 69–70, 91, 145
Schwarzenegger, Arnold, 70, 161
The Secret Life of Houdini, 233
See What Isn't There magnet, 127, 215–216
self-image, 173
Sex,Money, KISS, 12, 235
Shameless Exploitation, 234
sheds, backyard, example, 20
Sherlock Holmes, 104, 189
Sidis, Dr., and Sidis Method, 189, 233
Simmons, Gene, 12, 69, 71–72, 235
Simmons, Richard, 101, 182
Snowball, 101, 232
speaker
    professional, 52

and what you speak,
65–66, 68
speaking, misunderstand-
ing of, 109
speed-to-market, 185
spiritual beliefs and pros-
perity, 189
Spiritual Selling Tools, 239
Stag Party, 104
Stanley, Thomas, 169
Starbuck's, 103, 213
Start With No, 165
Steak 'n' Ale restaurants, 128
Stewart, Martha, 100, 101,
128
Stone, W. Clement, 57, 190,
192
The Strangest Secret, 234
strategy
asking as, 119
marketing, 47, 52, 207
place, 79, 80
pace and, 187
secrets of, 91
Success Is An Inside Job, 56,
239
Success magazine, 57
Success Motivation
Institute, 143
The Success Principles, 58
*The Success System That
Never Fails*, 57
*Success Through a Positive
Mental Attitude*, 57
Sugarman, Joe, 129
Sunrise Safari, 19
Sun Securities, 110
"Synchromatics" (Kramer),
170

T
"Takeaway Selling," 83
taxes, 35–36
Taxicab Confessions, 86
teleseminars, 121, 224
Terry and the Pirates
comic strip, 104
Texas Bix Bender, 80
"Thank–U–Gram," 170

Think and Grow Rich, 59,
63, 172, 233
Think Outside the Box, 91, 236
Thomas, Justice Clarence,
200
*Thoughts of Chairman
Buffett*, 232
thrift, 46
Tighe, John Francis, 73
"time vampires," 176
timing, 190
To Be or Not To Be Intimidated,
83
Tomshack, Dr. Chris, 61–62,
87, 238
Town & Country magazine, 17
Trump, Donald, 54, 67–68,
69, 76–77, 96–97, 105,
119, 161–162, 178, 185,
235
Trump, Ivanka, 67, 69, 71,
96–97
*Trump Strategies for Real
Estate* , 235
trustworthiness, 116
Tubbergen, Dennis, 62, 238
Turner, Glenn, 9, 235–236
*20 Ads That Shook the
World*, 133–135
Twitchell, 133
Tyson, Mike, 55

U
*The Ultimate Guidebook for
the Successful Gentleman*,
213
"The Ultimate Information
Entrepreneur's
Collection," 89
Ultimate Success Secret, 239
Unfinished Business, 22
Unlock The Game®, 238

V
value
and equity, 155, 156
personal, 150–154
Vance, Mike, 91, 176, 236
The Verdict movie, 13
Victoria's Secret, 19, 103

W
Wal-Mart, 129
Walton, Sam, 42
Warren Buffett Speaks, 232
wealth, 3, 156, 158
attitude about, 22
courage to attract, 181
creation, 42, 51, 112
inhibition, 7–8, 11
movement, seeking, 84
obstacles to, 175–177
passion for, 126
post-recession, 47
and rarity, 112
replaceable, 43
respect for, 144
speaking language of, 66
Wealth Account, 169–172
Wealth Attraction Coaching
Groups, 18–19
Wealth Attraction System, 156
wealth magnets (HPU), 199
"wealth seminars," 168–169
wealthy people,15–16
webinars, Glazer-Kennedy
University, 232
Winfrey, Oprah, 120
*Winning Through
Intimidation*, 83
Women With Balls, 182
work ethic, 65
work-money link, 65
Worth magazine, 17
Wrangell, George, 133–134
Wright, Frank Lloyd, 42
Wyland, Robert, 28

Y
YCDBSOYA, 77
YouTube marketing, 79

Z
Zehme, Bill, 102, 105
Ziglar, Zig, 10, 236
Zufelt, Jack M., 93

Special Opportunity for Readers of "No B.S.® Wealth Attraction For Entrepreneurs"...

The Most Incredible
FREE Gift Ever
($613.91 Worth of Pure Money-Making Information)

Dan Kennedy & Bill Glazer are offering an incredible opportunity for you to see WHY <u>Glazer-Kennedy Insider's Circle™ is known as "THE PLACE" where entrepreneurs seeking FAST and Dramatic Growth and greater Control, Independence, and Security come together.</u> Dan & Bill want to give you **$613.91 worth of pure Money-Making Information** including TWO months as an 'Elite' Gold Member of Glazer-Kennedy's Insider's Circle™. You'll receive a steady stream of MILLIONAIRE Maker Information including:

* Glazer-Kennedy University: Series of 3 Webinars (Value = $387.00)

The 10 "BIG Breakthroughs in Business Life with Dan Kennedy
- HOW <u>Any</u> Entrepreneur or Sales Professional can Multiply INCOME by 10X
- **HOW to Avoid Once and for All being an *"Advertising Victim"***
- The *"<u>Hidden Goldmine</u>"* in Everyone's Business and HOW to Capitalize on it
- **The BIGGEST MISTAKE most Entrepreneurs make in their Marketing**
- And the <u>BIGGEE</u>…Getting Customers Seeking You Out.

The ESSENTIALS to Writing Million Dollar Ads & Sales Letters BOTH
Online & Offline with *Marketing & Advertising Coach, Bill Glazer*
- How to INCREASE the Selling Power of <u>All</u> Your Advertising by Learning the <u>13 "Must Have" Direct Response Principles</u>
- **Key Elements that Determine the Success of Your Website**
- **HOW to Craft a Headline the Grabs the Reader's Attention**
- **How to Create an Irresistible Offer that Melts Away <u>Any</u> Resistance to Buy**
- The <u>Best</u> Ways to Create Urgency and Inspire IMMEDIATE Response
- *"Insider Strategies"* to INCREASE Response that you <u>Must</u> be using both ONLINE & Offline

The ESSENTIALS of Productivity & Implementation for Entrepreneurs w/
Peak Performance Coach Lee Milteer
- How to Almost INSTANTLY be MORE Effective, Creative, Profitable, and Take MORE Time Off
- **HOW to Master the "Inner Game" of Personal Peak Productivity**
- How to Get MORE Done in Less Time
- **HOW to Get Others to Work On <u>Your</u> Schedule**
- How to Create Clear Goals for SUCESSFUL Implementation
- And Finally the BIGGEE…How to Stop Talking and Planning Your Dreams and Start Implementing Them into Reality

* 'Elite' Gold Insider's Circle Membership (Two Month Value = $99.94):

- Two Issues of *The No B.S.® Marketing Letter:*

  Each issue is at least 12 pages – usually MORE – Overflowing with **the latest Marketing & MoneyMaking Strategies**. Current members refer to it as <u>a day-long intense seminar in print</u>, arriving by first class mail every month. There are ALWAYS terrific examples of *"What's-Working-NOW"* **Strategies**, timely Marketing news, trends, ongoing teaching of <u>Dan Kennedy's Most IMPORTANT Strategies</u>… and MORE. As soon as it arrives in your mailbox you'll want to find a quiet place, grab a highlighter, and devour every word.

- Two CDs Of The **EXCLUSIVE GOLD AUDIO INTERVIEWS**

  These are EXCLUSIVE interviews with <u>successful users of direct response advertising, leading experts and entrepreneurs in direct marketing, and famous business authors and speakers</u>. Use them to turn commuting hours into "POWER Thinking" hours.

  ### * The New Member No B.S.® Income Explosion Guide & CD (Value = $29.97)

  This resource is <u>especially designed for NEW MEMBERS</u> to show them HOW they can join the thousands of Established Members **creating exciting sales and PROFIT growth** in their Business, Practices, or Sales Careers & Greater SUCCESS in their Business lives.

  ### Income Explosion FAST START Tele-Seminar with Dan Kennedy, Bill Glazer, and Lee Milteer (Value = $97.00)
  Attend from the privacy and comfort of your home or office…hear a DYNAMIC discussion <u>of Key Advertising, Marketing, Promotion, Entrepreneurial & Phenomenon strategies</u>, PLUS answers to the most Frequently Asked Questions about these Strategies

* You'll also get these Exclusive "Members Only" Perks:

- **Special FREE Gold Member CALL-IN TIMES:** Several times a year, Dan & I schedule Gold-Member ONLY Call-In times
- **Gold Member RESTRICTED ACCESS WEBSITE**: Past issues of the *No B.S.® Marketing Letter*, articles, special news, etc.
- **Continually Updated MILLION DOLLAR RESOURCE DIRECTORY** with Contacts and Resources Dan & his clients use.

To activate your MOST INCREDIBLE FREE GIFT EVER you only pay a one-time charge of $19.95 (or $39.95 for Int'l subscribers) to cover postage (this is for everything). **After your 2-Month FREE test-drive, you will automatically continue at the <u>lowest</u> Gold Member price of $49.97 per month ($59.97 outside North America). Should you decide to cancel your membership, you can do so at any time by calling Glazer-Kennedy Insider's Circle™ at 410-825-8600 or faxing a cancellation note to 410-825-3301 (Monday through Friday 9am – 5pm). Remember, your credit card will NOT be charged the low monthly membership fee until the beginning of the 3rd month, which means you will receive 2 full issues to read, test, and profit from all of the powerful techniques and strategies you get from being an Insider's Circle Gold Member. And of course, it's impossible for you to lose, because if you don't absolutely LOVE everything you get, you can simply cancel your membership before the third month and never get billed a single penny for membership.**

EMAIL REQUIRED IN ORDER TO NOTIFY YOU ABOUT THE GLAZER-KENNEDY UNIVERSITY WEBINARS AND FAST START TELESEMINAR

Name _____ Business Name _____

Address _____

City _____ State _____ Zip _____ e-mail* _____

Phone _____ Fax _____

Credit Card Instructions to Cover $19.95 for Shipping & Handling:

_____Visa _____MasterCard _____ American Express _____ Discover

Credit Card Number _____ Exp. Date _____

Signature _____ Date _____

FAX BACK TO 410-825-3301
Or mail to: 401 Jefferson Ave., Towson, MD 21286
www.In12Months.com